A
Woman's
Mitzvah

A Fully Sourced Guide to the Laws of Family Purity

A
Woman's
Mitzvah

Meira Svirsky

*Based on Classes
by Rav Yitzchak Berkovits, שליט״א*

*Halachic Sources Provided
by Rav Yirmiyohu Kaganoff, שליט״א*

Jerusalem

2019

Cover Artwork: Claire Ciss

מאירה סבירסקי
מצוה של אשה
ספר על הלכות טהרת המשפחה
בשפה אנגלית
עטיפה: קלייר סיס
עיצוב: ברוך-אלכסנדר פלוחוטנקו
מודפס בבית דפוס ״העיר העתיקה בע״מ״: רח׳ בית הדפוס 30, גבעת שאול, י-ם
טל׳: 666-1999 (02), 666-1943, פקס 652-1029. oldcity@netvision.net.il

© 2007, כל זכויות שמורות למאירה סבירסקי

Meira Svirsky
A WOMAN'S MITZVAH
Book about the Laws of Family Purity
Cover Artwork: Claire Ciss
Book Design: Barukh-Alexander Plokhotenko
Printed in Israel by Old City, Ltd.

Third Printing, 2019

ISBN: 978-965722-724-4

Published by
Ktav Publishing House
527 Empire Blvd
Brooklyn, NY 11225
www.ktav.com | orders@ktav.com
(718) 972-5449

This book is dedicated
in loving memory to

JUDITH DAN, z'l

יהודית מרים בת העארש צבי ז"ל

Her warmth, dignity and inner spiritual strength
distinguished her
as an *aishes chayil* and made her
an example to everyone.

Dedicated by Her Loving Children and Grandchildren

This book is dedicated
to the *ilui neshamah*
of our dear mother

CHAYA BAS TZVI HALEVI
(MRS. KLARA KEST), *z'l*
חיה בת צבי הלוי ז"ל

We were privileged to be children
of this true *aishes chayil*
who wholeheartedly dedicated her life
to *Torah* and the welfare of her family.

Ezra and Leah Kest

This book is dedicated
in honor of our dear mother

MRS. ROCHELLE DINA BROOKS

May *Hashem* continue to bless
her with the strength
to continue all her good work and the merit
to receive abundant *nachas*
from her children and grandchildren.

Ezra and Leah Kest

This book is dedicated
in honor of our holy mothers

MARIOSA BAT ZELDA
(MARILYN FOX)

ROCHEL BAT CHAVA
(RUTH CLAMAN)

In gratitude for your unending efforts
to connect us to truth,
dignity and holiness.
May *Hashem* bless you until 120 years
to see the fruits of your dedicated energy
towards creating the next generation of our People.

With eternal love,
Aba and Pamela Claman

This book is dedicated
in loving memory
to the *ilui neshamah*
of my dear uncle who, despite his illness,
was always a source of inspiration and humor

DOV BER BEN SHMUEL, z'l

דוב בער בן שמואל ז״ל

and in honor of my grandmothers

MIRIAM BIDA
HELA FLEISCHER

Jennifer Melzer

Rabbi Yitzchak Berkovits
Sanhedria HaMurchevet 113/27
Jerusalem, Israel 97707
02-5813847

יצחק שמואל הלוי ברקוביץ
ראש רשת כוללים לינת הצדק
סנהדרייה המורחבת 113/27
ירושלם ת״ו

Bs"d Jerusalem, 3 Menachem Av, 5779

As Mrs. Svirsky's A Woman's Mitzvah goes to print for the third time, I wish to express my satisfaction in it's having become a sourcebook for Kallah instructors around the globe. The author has herself earned her reputation as a transmitter of Torah values with depth of understanding and deep-felt emotion, and that is very much reflected in this work.

The classes this book is based on were given to a select group of women expected at the time to be dedicating their lives to the Klal. Mrs. Svirsky has over the years brought the magic of Taharas Hamishpacha to so many women who otherwise struggled with various aspects of the mitzvah and married life in general. The sensitivity and life experience dating back to the days the book was written are clearly detectable in the style and content and I am sure many more kallah instructors can greatly benefit from this work.

May the author continue to introduce women to the wealth of Torah family life both in person and with the printed word.

Bivracha,

Yitzchak Berkovits

Tishrei 5768 / October 2007

FOUNDER & DEAN
Rabbi Noah Weinberg

DAN FAMILY OF CANADA
WORLD CENTER
Jerusalem, Israel

AISH PROGRAMS
Aish.com
Aishaudio.com
Aish on Campus
Aish Productions
Discovery Production
EYAHT
Essentials
Executive Learning Center
Hasbara Fellowships
HonestReporting
Jerusalem Fellowships
Jerusalem Partners
JEWEL
Jewish Family Institute
Project Chazon
Russian Program
SpeedDating®
Spanish Division
The Jerusalem Fund
Yeshivat Aish HaTorah

AISH BRANCHES
Ashdod, Israel
Baltimore
Bat Yam, Israel
Birmingham, UK
Boston
Cleveland
Denver
Detroit
Essex, UK
Jerusalem, Israel
Johannesburg, SA
Kiev, Ukraine
Las Vegas
Livingston, NJ
London
Los Angeles
Manchester, UK
Melbourne, Australia
New York
Petach Tikva, Israel
Philadelphia
Santiago, Chile
Sao Paulo, Brazil
Scottsdale, AZ
Seattle
South Florida
St. Louis
Toronto
Washington, DC
Winnipeg, CA

Mrs. Meira Svirsky has been a long time and very successful educator and teacher in the various Aish HaTorah programs. Many topics that cover the scope of Judaism have been covered by her expertise knowledge.

She set for herself to write a *sefer* on the *halachos* and *hashkafah* of the Laws of Family Purity, *Taharas HaMishpacha*. The result turned out magnificent! A very clear and important *sefer* came out after many years of effort that covers all aspects of these laws from beginning to end. Both the unfamiliar and the teacher of these laws will benefit greatly from learning and teaching from this book. The fact that it has been written by a woman for women makes it into an even more useful *sefer* that will penetrate both the mind and heart of those who delve into it.

I heartfully recommend this *sefer* both for its unique approach and practical explanations it contains.

This letter also serves as my recommendation as to Mrs. Svirsky's teachings. She has proven herself as a clear spokeswoman for the Jewish people.

I wish Mrs. Meira Svirsky much *hatzlachah* and *brachah* in all her undertakings.

Noah Weinberg
Rav Noah Weinberg
Rosh HaYeshiva
Aish HaTorah

One Western Wall Plaza ● POB 14149 ● Old City, Jerusalem, Israel
Tel: (972-2) 628-5666 ● Fax: (972-2) 627-3172 ● Email: Jerusalem@aish.com ● www.aish.com

Rav Yirmiyohu Kaganoff

3 Kfar Ivri, Neve Yaakov

Jerusalem, Israel

Author of three volumes
on Meleches Shabbos *Nimla Tal*

Formerly Rav of Congregation
Darchei Tzedek; Baltimore, MD

Rosh Kollel of Beis Yisroel Yeshivah

Rav in Neve Yaakov, Yerushalayim

לוי ירמיהו הכהן כהנוב (קגנוף)

קפר עברי 3, נוה יעקב

י-ם, ישראל

מחייס ״נמלא טל״ על מלאכות
שבת ג׳׳ח

מלפנים רב דק׳׳ק דרכי צדק
בלטימור, מרילנד

ראש כולל בית ישראל ישיבה

מו׳׳צ בשכונת נוה יעקב, י-ם

Tishrei 5768/October 2007

Over many years, Meira Svirsky has put her experience at teaching *kallos* to good service in producing a very readable and highly informative book on the laws and *hashkafos* of Jewish family life for women by a woman.

Several years back, she asked me if I could provide the references for the book and check it for accuracy, which I have attempted to do very carefully. I believe that the *halachos* in this book are accurate.

I have thoroughly enjoyed the years of working with Mrs. Svirsky on this project, in which at times I almost felt like a co-collaborator. I wish her much *nachas* from her family and her students, both those she meets and those who read her book, and am looking forward to seeing her future endeavors.

<h1>Table of Contents</h1>

♦

Acknowledgments

I would like to express my deepest gratitude to my *rabbanim* and teachers, Rav Yitzchak Berkovits and Rav Yirmiyohu Kaganoff. *Hashem* should bless them to inspire many more generations with their *avodas hakodesh*.

This book was based on classes given by Rav Berkovits, whose clarity of approach and understanding of *halachah* is recognized by his thousands of students worldwide. To Rav Berkovits, my teacher over many years, I owe all of the fruits of my teaching, writing and years of *mitzvah* observance.

Rav Kaganoff took on the enormous job of providing sources for every *halachah* cited in this book. In addition, he understood my desire to understand the rulings of our Sages, *rishonim* and *achronim* and patiently provided me with much additional historical and *halachic* background information on many *halachos*, which I have included in this book. His breadth and depth of knowledge and dedication to accuracy can be found on every page. I have gained tremendous knowledge and inspiration from Rav Kaganoff. The merits gained from this book are also his.

I would also like to express my deep gratitude and thanks to Rav Noah Weinberg, *Rosh HaYeshivah* of *Aish HaTorah*, and Rebbetzin Denah Weinberg, dean and director of EYAHT for their wisdom, inspiration and vision, which they have imparted to me for so many years. Many blessings for their continued successs.

Many people helped make this book possible and lent their help to me through the process of writing, editing and production. My heartfelt blessings and thanks to Andrea and Stuart Hytman, Leah and Ezra Kest, and Pamela and Aba Claman for their generous support of this book. Many, many thanks also to Rabbi Eric

Coopersmith, Rebbetzin Dena Glaser, Rebbetzin Ruth Gluckin and Larry and Jennifer Melzer, who also generously supported this project.

My editors and proofreaders extended themselves and helped me in so many ways beyond their jobs. My gratitude is boundless to Rabbi Daniel Schloss for his many helpful suggestions, his excellent proofreading and his tireless efforts in helping me to complete the book. Also, my deepest thanks to Uriela Obst Sagiv, the book's first editor, and to David Noll, Abby Reading, Batya Kayman and Bracha Shor for their proofreading and their many helpful suggestions and tireless support. Many thanks to Claire Ciss for the artwork on the cover, to Rebbetzin Rivka Shore for the title of the book and to Barukh-Alexander and Rivka Plokhotenko for the technical production of the book and their endless devotion to this project.

The encouragement and help I received from my friends, students and fellow staff members of *Aish HaTorah Yeshivah* was crucial in helping me complete this project. My sincerest thanks to Tzivia Jesmer, Bracha Strauss, Devora Rabinowitz and Chaya Richmond of the *Aish HaTorah* staff and to Rebbetzin Dina Coopersmith, Rebbetzin Bruchie Coopersmith, Donna Abraham, Chana Gilman, Miriam Noll, Rebbetzin Bayla Berger, Eve Solomon, Hadassah Saks, Barbara and Eli Grossman, Heather Tzall and to the many more people who helped make this book possible.

My husband, Efim, is an endless source of light and support. Without his constant encouragement, this book would never have come to fruition. *Hashem* should continue to bless him with all good and the continued opportunity to share the tremendous gifts *Hashem* has given him. My parents and parents-in-law also have been a constant source of support and moral inspiration. To them, my gratitude is unending. May the strengthening of Jewish women through this book be a merit to the *neshomos* of my dear father, Henry Paskin, and mother-in-law, Paulina Svirsky, already in *Gan Eden*.

To all my students, who waited patiently for this book and continually encouraged me: You will never know how much I appreciate every one of you. To all of my students from the *Aish HaTorah Smichah Wives Program* who are now rebbetzins in *Aish* branches around the world: May this book help you in all your teaching and be a guide for all of your students.

ACKNOWLEDGMENTS

To my dear children — Avraham Simchah, Yonah Lev, Ahavah Rochel, Yosef Yehudah and Moshe Chaninah: May the light of *Torah* continue to shine upon you and guide you in all your endeavors.

To the Creator of the universe: Words are inadequate to express the gratitude and joy of being *zoche* to being able to keep your holy *Torah*. Your presence was evident in every aspect of this book.

Meira Svirsky

Tishrei 5768/October 2007
Jerusalem

♦

Author's Note

As women, we have been entrusted with the primary care of keeping the Laws of Family Purity. We are aware of the enormous importance of these laws which provide the foundation of the Jewish family. We know that we provide the link to the next generation of the Jewish people.

We are also aware of the enormous importance of these laws by considering the spiritual consequences of eschewing them,[1] and we want to get them right. Yet, in our desire to "do it right," we often needlessly make ourselves full of worry. Instead of being able to keep these commandments *b'simcha*, with happiness — in the spirit that *Hashem* wants us to keep all of His commandments — they become a source of anxiety and stress.

How does a woman keep these *mitzvos* properly, while at the same time live her life in a relaxed, positive manner? How can she be serious about all the details involved in these *mitzvos*, yet be free from anxiety that she is making mistakes? In addition to learning the practical applications of these laws, as women, we must be well versed in the principles behind the laws. This knowledge gives us the framework for "getting it right." Just as we would never be able to keep *Shabbos*

---

[1] It is interesting to note that the consequence for a couple who knowingly has relations during *niddah* is the same consequence given to someone who enters the *Beis HaMikdash*, the Temple, in a state of spiritual impurity. It is also the same consequence given for breaking *Shabbos*, eating on *Yom Kippur* and to a man who refuses to have a *bris milah* and enter into the convenant of God and the Jewish people. See Ch. 4 for more information.

properly without the knowledge and parameters of the 39 *melachos*, so too, we must be aware of the parameters of the Laws of Family Purity.

Educating ourselves in Jewish law has always been both an obligation and a pleasure for Jewish women. My experience teaching and counseling Jewish women about the Laws of Family Purity has shown me that the more women understand the principles behind these laws, the better the laws are kept. This knowledge also makes us more in tune to them — more questions are asked and fewer details are overlooked. With this education, comes peace of mind as well as an increased feeling of dignity.

It is my fervent hope that from the experience of keeping the Laws of Family Purity properly, Jewish women will experience first hand that "All its ways are pleasant."[2]

About This Book

A Woman's Mitzvah was written with both beginning and advanced "students" of the Laws of Family Purity in mind. In addition, if you are a teacher of this subject and need a well-sourced, yet readable guide, I hope you will find this book valuable.

The information in this book has been culled from lectures given by Rav Yitzchak Berkovits. Sources have been provided by Rav Yirmiyohu Kaganoff, who also re-viewed the book. Rav Kaganoff was also kind enough to provide me with much interesting background and historical information that I have included in the foot-notes.

Special attention has been given to distinguish between what is a law (*halachah*), what is a custom (*minhag*), and what is a stringency beyond the *halachic* require-ment (*chumrah*). In addition, topical discussions explaining the Jewish attitude to-wards marriage and intimacy have also been sourced and included in this book.

It is my deepest hope that those who follow the path of a Jewish marriage should find joy, fulfillment and personal growth through these commandments.

---

2   *Mishlei* 3:17.

CHAPTER 1

◆

What Is Meant by "Purity"

A basic misunderstanding of the Laws of Family Purity often centers around the very name "Family Purity." What is meant by "purity"?

The Hebrew noun *taharah* (or the adjective *tahor*) has no English equivalent. "Spiritual purity" may be the closest translation, but the concept means much more than those English words convey. *Taharah* refers to a state of existence that is purely spiritual and totally non-physical. It is not a value judgement of good or bad; it is also not a judgement of a person's worth.

It is significant to note that one can become *tamei*, spiritually impure, by fulfilling some of the greatest commandments, *mitzvos*, of the *Torah*. For example, a person taking care of a dead body — a *mitzvah* involving one of the greatest acts of kindness[1] — becomes *tamei*, spiritually impure, by doing so.[2]

In the times when the *Beis HaMikdash*, the Temple, stood in Jerusalem, the priests were instructed to prepare ashes of a red heifer, which were used for purifying the Jewish nation. By performing this *mitzvah*, the priests became *tamei*.[3]

While it is true that we always want to return to *taharah*, it is also true that our spiritual growth in this world involves a process. Sometimes this process takes us through a state of spiritual impurity.

---

[1] *Sotah* 14a.
[2] *Bamidbar* 9:6; 19:11.
[3] *Bamidbar* 19:7.

Since the *mitzvos* of the *Torah* are decreed by God alone and are a human being's vehicle for getting close to God (by doing His will), it cannot be that the worth of person who fulfills a commandment is anyway diminished, even if in the process he or she becomes *tamei*.

Spiritual Growth as a Process

Most sources of *tumah* result from death or the loss of potential life. Because death is the ultimate loss of the ability to exercise free will, it is also the ultimate loss of spiritual opportunity in this world.[4] Hence, a person who comes in contact with death is enjoined to "process" this experience so that it can be used for his or her spiritual growth. *Halachically*, one of the ways God has chosen to do this is to distance us from certain activities, creating a type of "spiritual space" to foster this growth.

Applicability

Many of the laws concerning spiritual purity and impurity revolve around an individual's ability to enter the *Beis HaMikdash*. Hence, without the *Beis HaMikdash*, they have no applicability today. There are, however, two basic areas of applicability of these laws in our times:

- ✦ The prohibition against contact with the dead for a man who is a *kohen*, a descendant of the priestly line (except under certain cirsumstances), and,

- ✦ The prohibition against physical contact between a hus-

---

[4]   Thus, the death of a human being respresents the greatest amount of *tumah*, since, when alive, a human being possesses the greatest potential for the manifestation of God's presence in the world. Significantly, a woman after birth becomes *tamei*, since the potential for life which was previously inside her is no longer with her. If she has given birth to a girl, her state of *tumah* is twice as long as that for a boy. Since a girl possesses within her the potential to bear life, the departure of a baby girl represents a loss of twice the potential as that of a boy. (As heard from Rav Yitzchak Berkovits.)

band and wife while the wife is *niddah*, or separate. This separation begins from the onset of a woman's menstrual cycle (or any other time of bleeding caused by the shedding of the lining of the uterus). Although on a smaller scale than the above example, this is also associated with a loss of life or potential life.

Unlike many societies that stigmatize women during their mentrual cycle, the Jewish attitude on the subject is vastly different. Judaism considers it normal, natural and healthy that women go through this cycle. Specifically, the required separation during this time is considered the best possible avenue for spiritual growth — both for men and women — due to the realities of our life as mortals in a finite world. (This idea is discussed in depth in the following chapter.) Moreover, Judaism demands that, rather than ignoring the biological ebbs and flows of our bodies, we use this vital information to foster our growth. This is why the Laws of Family Purity affect not just the woman, but the entire family, in a multi-faceted way.

Clearly, the name "Family Purity" is no coincidence or euphemism. On the most apparent level, keeping these laws is considered the key to a good marriage — a marriage that is vital, alive and constantly renewing itself. Anyone who has been around a couple who has such a marriage cannot help but notice how their positive relationship affects their children and others around them.

On a metaphysical level, the *Gemara*[5] tells us when a couple keeps these laws, they also positively affect the spiritual world, namely, through the souls of the children born to them. (See Ch. 9 for a further discussion of this issue.)

The Process at Work

From the time a woman's period (or any other blood originating from the shedding of the uterine lining) begins, she and her husband cease having any

---

[5] *Nedarim* 20b.

physical contact. This separation lasts a minimum of twelve days. (The separation is longer if the woman's period or the bleeding lasts longer than five days.) After this time, the woman immerses herself in a *mikveh*, a "ritual bath," and the couple resumes their physical relationship.

One of the reasons the Hebrew word *mikveh* is translated as "ritual" bath is because a *mikveh* has nothing to do with the usual sort of bath we all take when we are dirty. Indeed, Jewish law tells us that a woman must be scrupulously clean *before* immersing in a *mikveh*, so that the waters of the *mikveh* will reach every part of her body.

Hence, it is clear that the waters of the *mikveh* have nothing to do with "cleanliness" on a physical level. Rather, the purpose of immersing in a *mikveh* is to change one's spiritual status. Although the medium through which a *mikveh* accomplishes this change is water, the change occurs on a strictly spiritual level.

And it is through this meeting — of the physical and the spiritual — that we are given the ability, as human beings in a finite world, to affirm and touch Infinite Reality.

♦

CHAPTER 2

The Laws of Family Purity — A View From the Beginning of Time

To start at the beginning in Judaism means to start in the Garden of Eden. And we must return there to begin understanding the Laws of Family Purity — why they are eternally relevant, and why they are particularly relevant in the times we find ourselves today.

The modern world has devoted much energy to the "problem" of boredom in marital relations — both emotional and physical. Self-help books, expert opinions and even media attention are constantly devoted to this subject. As society has become more "open" and values more "liberal," innovations have abounded to try to solve this problem.

Yet all of the modern world's cures have failed abysmally. Divorce rates are higher than ever and climbing, as is general dissatisfaction regarding the state of male-female relationships.

Why Do We Get Bored?

The modern world has been unable to provide an adequate answer to this problem. So let us go back to the Garden of Eden, where the Jewish answer is found and its system for *tikun*, "repair," was instituted.

The Turning Point:
Knowledge of Good and Evil

The moment Adam and Eve ate from the Tree of Knowledge of Good and Evil, a fundamental change occurred in the world, both in body and spirit. Before the sin in the Garden, body and mind — physicality and spirituality — were completely united in purpose.

Rav Eliyahu Dessler in *Michtav Mei'Eliyahu* explains that before the sin, evil stood outside of mankind, hence the first people saw the world only in terms of what was true and what was false.[1] Man was completely permeated with good and hence only saw "life with one reality: a life with God. All else was false, unreal, illusory."[2]

After the sin, evil became perceptible to mankind from within. This condition fostered a tremendous drop in the state of mankind. Rav Dessler explains: "We feel that evil is as real as good. We can imagine ourselves living a life where we reject God, as so many do. We realize this would be wrong, of course, but we see it could be a successful life in many ways. This is what is meant above by our seeing both good and evil as real."[3]

Before the sin, when good entirely permeated man, his physicality was also completely driven by the desire to do good. Thus, the physical served and enhanced the spiritual. It was one of our means of getting closer to and becoming one with God.

After the sin, it became possible to use the physical as an end in itself, as a means to accomplish something completely devoid of good and devoid of spirituality. With evil now inside us, desires for base pleasures — regardless of their harmfulness — emanated from the inside of mankind.[4] And in no other realm was this more pronounced than in the realm of intimacy. The *Torah* tells us that

---

[1]   Rabbi Eliyahu E. Dessler, *Strive for Truth, Bereishis.*
[2]   Ibid, pg. 14.
[3]   Ibid.
[4]   Sforno on *Bereishis* 3:7.

the first thing Adam and Eve did after eating from the Tree of Knowledge of Good and Evil was to make for themselves clothing to cover their bodies. Why did this suddenly become important to them? Before the sin, the *Torah* relates, Adam and Eve were "naked and not ashamed."[5] But now "the eyes of both of them were opened, and they realized they were naked; and they sewed together a fig leaf and made themselves aprons."[6]

What does it mean that their eyes were opened? Rashi tells us that this "opening" of their eyes is not to be taken literally. Rather, it refers to a new-found intelligence and awareness.[7] Similarly, Rambam and Ramban explain that this "opening" had to do with receiving new sources of knowledge, not the physical sense of sight. As Rashi notes,[8] even a blind person knows that he is naked!

Moreover, the *Torah* makes a point to tell us that before the sin when they were naked, they were not ashamed, implying that after the sin, they were.

Rav Shimshon Raphael Hirsch explains, "They had become enlightened people. But their first realization was — that they were naked ... As long as man stands completely in the service of his God, he has no reason to be ashamed of any part of his body ... But when this condition is not entirely there, he feels shame [in his nakedness].[9]

After the sin, mankind was able to see that it could use the body not only as a vehicle for the soul but also for its own selfish purposes. Namely, Adam and Eve saw, with clarity and for the first time, the possibility of discarding the soul as an equal partner with the body in intimate relations — essentially, using another person for selfish purposes. It was this new attitude toward their physicality that made them ashamed of their nakedness. As Hirsch explains, "The shame came to awaken the voice within us, which is intimately connected to the conscience that reminds us we are not meant to be animals."[10]

---

[5]   *Bereishis* 2:25.
[6]   *Bereishis* 3:7.
[7]   Rashi on *Bereishis* 3:7.
[8]   *Bereishis Rabbah* on 3:7, quoted by Rashi ad loc.
[9]   Hirsch on *Bereishis* 3:7.
[10]   Ibid.

The Advent of Mortality

A careful look at all of the consequences given to Adam and Eve for eating from the Tree of Knowledge reveals that each consequence addresses a different aspect of the new state of mankind's physicality. Although these consequences are referred to as curses, in reality, they provide the path to repair, *tikun*, in our post-Garden of Eden world.[11] Even death, the ultimate consequence of the sin, is a blessing, since we would otherwise be doomed to be eternally imperfect.[12]

The *Gemara* relates that one of the most basic aspects of being mortal is that we forget.[13] We forget emotions; we forget what we have learned. In short, without some kind of a structure to remind us, we can forget why we are here.

When we forget our true purpose in this world, boredom sets in, trying to convince us that we need something new, something exciting — even forbidden — to spark life anew. Yet rather than accomplish this purpose, we soon tire of these new pursuits, requiring something even more exotic to excite us. Nowhere is this process more evident than in the realm of intimacy. As boredom and the desire for the exotic set in, the physical is fed at the expense of the spiritual, leading us further and further from reality and one of our true goals — creating a vibrant, long-term bond of unity between husband and wife. On the other hand, a structure that reminds us of our purpose in life exerts a certain type of pressure on us (without which, things go off track pretty fast). Just as it is a law of the physical world that all life decomposes when left alone, so, too in our spiritual life. The guidelines provided by the *Torah* counteract this basic law of nature.[14]

The Laws of Family Purity, a system that requires a couple to refrain from their physical relationship at certain times, help assure that a couple doesn't get

---

[11] As heard from Rebbetzin Tzipporah Heller.

[12] Death comes as an atonement for certain sins that we would otherwise have no means of which to rid ourselves. *Yoma* 85b.

[13] *Yerushalmi Peah* 1:1.

[14] See *Niddah* 31b, where Rebbi Meir says that the purpose of the seven days of separation is so that the wife should be as beloved to her husband as when she stood under their *chupah*.

bored with one another. The times forge new levels of intimacy by fostering the husband and wife's emotional and spiritual connection.

The new levels of intimacy created by these connections infuse their physical relationship with ever-increasing levels of closeness, as well as a freshness that results from the separation. Because this process increases the emotional and spiritual closeness of a couple over time, their physical relationship takes on an ever-deepening spiritual and emotional component.

Despite the powerful drives of the body in our post-Garden of Eden world, relating to another human being strictly as a body can never be ultimately satisfying. Since we are both body and soul, every aspect of our lives must be infused with the appropriate partnership between these two parts. In truth, physical intimacy is not about a body relating to another body; it is about a soul relating to another soul through the *medium* of the body.

Creating Unity

Let us look at the language used by the *Torah* to describe physical intimacy.

"Now the man had known his wife, Eve, and she conceived."[15] The concept of knowledge encompasses communication and understanding. Thus the *Torah* teaches that the love between a husband and wife is connected with these concepts.[16]

"And God said, it is not good that man should be alone, I will make him a help mate opposite him[17]... Therefore a man shall leave his father and mother and cling to his wife, and they shall become one flesh."[18]

Commenting on these verses, Hirsch gives us the following insight, "As long as the man was alone, it was not yet 'good.' Once the division had been made, it was no longer possible for man to fulfill his calling by himself ... without her, he

---

[15]   *Bereishis* 4:1.
[16]   As heard from Rav Yitzchak Berkovits. See also *HaEmek Davar* on *Bereishis* 4:1.
[17]   *Bereishis* 2:20.
[18]   *Bereishis* 2:24.

was only half a man ... after [their] reunion, man and woman become one single body."[19]

Hirsch explains what this union is, how it can be achieved, and why human beings are unique among all living beings:

"But [this union] can only take place if, at the same time, they become one mind, one heart, one soul. But that can only take place if they subordinate all their strengths and efforts, all their thoughts and desires to the service of a Higher Will. And herein lies the great difference between the sexual life of all other living creatures and that of a human marriage.

"All the rest of the living [animal] world is divided into sexes. But in their case both sexes sprang independently from the earth. They do not require each other for the fulfillment of their life's calling, and only for the purpose of breeding, and for the time necessary for perpetuating the species, do they seek and find each other. But the human female is part of the human male ... man is helpless and lacking independence without his wife. Only the two together form a complete human being. Life in its entirety, in every phase, demands their union. Only of man does it say, 'and he should cleave to his wife.' "[20]

Fundamentally, the *Torah* intends a husband and wife to be unified on every level, from the spiritual to the emotional to the physical.[21] Physical intimacy is a reflection of the harmony that a couple strives to feel in every aspect of their lives together. In its perfected state, physical intimacy is the natural completion of a couple's intense spiritual and emotional connection.[22]

This is the goal of every couple, Judaism tells us — to work toward the type of relationship where each spouse's intense feelings of love for the other motivate the desire for physical relations. Rather than relations taking care of one's physical desires, the desire for relations emanates from a couple's longing to become

---

19   Hirsch on *Bereishis* 2:24.
20   Ibid.
21   Rav Yitzchak Berkovits, explaining Ramban on *Bereishis* 2:24.
22   As heard from Rav Yitzchak Berkovits.

one with each other.[23] Ultimately, the harmony that is felt in marital relations is an expression of how the relationship is at all times.

To achieve this level of a relationship takes a lot of time and effort. The Jewish idea of a good marriage necessarily means that the best memories of the marriage are not from the first years, but rather from the later years — years that bear the fruits of each partner's investment in understanding, helping and learning to love the other. It is this investment that makes a couple operate as a unit and truly feel one with one another.

Yet, intimacy is not a *mitzvah* limited to the "perfected marriage." It is a *mitzvah* that begins when the marriage begins and evolves and develops over time. The many *kavannos*, intentions, listed by the Code of Jewish Law regarding intimacy attest to this.[24] God, in His wisdom, gave us a *mitzvah* — that of creating oneness between husband and wife. Intimacy is one of the means He created to help us fulfill that *mitzvah*.[25]

A Dynamic Marriage

Judaism views as a responsibility of every couple to make their marriage a

---

[23] *Sidur Beis Yaakov* (of Rav Yaakov Emden), *Hanhagos Leil Shabbos* 7:2:6.

[24] *Orach Chayim* 240.

[25] As heard from Rav Yitzchak Berkovits: The role of the physical relationship, before a couple realizes what its true purpose is all about — [namely] surrender, trust, unity — is to build that relationship and come closer to that goal. It is an expression of intent (to create such a relationship) and an expression of commitment (to do whatever it takes to feel this unity and sense of selflessness). During this entire period, the couple is not fooling themselves. They know this is not the ultimate relationship, but in everything they do, they have in mind the goal of one day feeling this sense of oneness and are committed to doing whatever it takes to get there. The physical relationship is an expression of that commitment. This is also very meaningful.

During these earlier stages in a marriage, the physical relationship is merely an expression of where the couple is striving. Its true importance is that there is nothing else in the relationship that is making this statement in such strong and powerful terms. Everything else that is going on in the relationship at that time can be considered learning to coexist — not achieving this level of unity, selflessness, trust and surrender. However, any intent without action does not achieve anything. So, the action of being together is the action that brings us closer to our goal of becoming a unit.

dynamic oneness. The systems it offers are the Laws of Family Purity and the laws which comprise the commandments between *adam l'chaveiro*, between "man and man,"[26] in this case, between husband and wife.

The Laws of Family Purity direct a couple not to take each other for granted; moreover, they create an awareness of the different stages of the wife's body. It is precisely this awareness that sets the tone for the marriage.[27]

These stages are traditionally seen as the two types of relationships that exist in a marriage: At times husband and wife relate to each other as husband and wife and at other times as brother and sister.

This idea is expressed in one of the most poetic of Jewish texts, the *Song of Songs* by King Solomon:[28]

How fair was your love in so many settings,
My sister, O bride;
So superior is your love to wine.

A sister and brother are so close that they cannot marry. This relationship is likened to the couple's relationship during the time of physical separation. It is a time to step back and see themselves and their spouse as individuals, while at the same time relating to each other in a way that develops ever deepening levels of understanding and closeness. During the days of togetherness, the couple reconnects with each other with this added dimension of closeness, creating ever deepening levels of unity with each cycle of togetherness.

Both parts of the cycle are needed to create the necessary dynamics. Taken together with the level of sensitivity and understanding demanded by the laws between man and man, it is a system that works.

---

[26] Literally, between man and his friend. There are two groups of laws in Judaism: Those between man and God and those between man and his fellow man.
[27] As heard from Rav Yitzchak Berkovits.
[28] *Shir HaShirim* 4:10.

CHAPTER 3

◆

What Is Niddah?

Let us begin by defining *niddah* and its conditions. *Niddah* literally means "separate." It is the word used to describe the time of physical separation between a husband and wife. Typically, a woman becomes *niddah* — that is, becomes separate from her husband — when she has her period or after giving birth.[1] Observing this separation is a *mitzvah*, a commandment, of the *Torah*.[2]

Based on the verses in the *Torah* where this *mitzvah* is mentioned, the *Gemara*[3] provides a very precise definition of what makes a woman *niddah* according to *Torah* law, including many insights into the specific laws, or *halachos*, of this very

---

[1] Technically, a woman becomes a *yoledes* after giving birth. However, in our days, since the *taharah* process for a *yoledes* is the same as that of a *niddah*, we will use the the term *niddah* for any time a woman and her husband must separate.

[2] "Do not come near a woman during her period of uncleanness to uncover her nakedness." (*Vayikra* 18:19.) "When a woman has a discharge — her discharge being blood from her body — she remains in her separation for seven days ... When she ceases her flow, she counts seven days; and afterwards, she can be purified." (*Vayikra* 15:19–28.) "When a woman conceives and gives birth to a male, she shall be unclean seven days as the days of her menstrual flow ... if she gives birth to a female, she shall be unclean two weeks as during her menstruation." (*Vayikra* 12:1–5.)

[3] The *Gemara* is the recording of the discussions of the *yeshivos* in Babylonia and Israel that took place roughly 1,700–1,800 years ago. The decisions reached in the *halachic* parts of these discussions are binding on all Jews as absolute *halachah* (Rambam, Introduction to *Mishneh Torah*).

important area of Jewish life.[4] The *Gemara* also details essential guidelines so that a husband and wife do not separate unnecessarily, yet properly observe the laws of *niddah*. To keep these laws faithfully, it is important to understand these guidelines, as well as the three conditions of *niddah* as defined in the *Gemara*, which we will discuss below.

The Three Conditions of Niddah

A woman becomes *niddah* by *Torah* law when all of the following three conditions are fulfilled:

1. Blood of a specific color left the uterus through the cervix;[5]
2. The blood did not come from a wound;[6]
3. A *hargashah* was experienced.[7]

We will now discuss each of these conditions in detail.

1. Blood of a Specific Color Left the Uterus Through the Cervix

For a woman to become *niddah*, the blood must leave the uterus through the cervix. The cervix is the narrow, neck-like, outer end of the uterus which opens into the vagina. It is precisely when the blood leaves the cervix that a woman becomes *niddah*; that is, the blood need not have left the body, only the cervix.[8]

Furthermore, according to the *Mishnah*,[9] for the blood to be considered *niddah*

---

[4]   A woman may also become *niddah* through rabbinic law. See the section *Special Circumstances: Finding a Stain While Not Niddah* at the end of this chapter.

[5]   *Niddah* 21b.

[6]   *Niddah* 16a.

[7]   *Niddah* 3a.

[8]   *Niddah* 57b; *Rambam, Hilchos Issurei Bi'ah* 5:2. Some *halachic* authorities contend that even after the blood has left the cervix, a woman does not become *niddah* until the blood arrives at an area that can be reached with a *bedikah* cloth.

[9]   *Niddah* 19a. When the *Torah* was given to the Jewish people at Mount Sinai, we were given two components: The written *Torah*, and its extensive orally transmitted commentary, called the Oral Law. This Oral Law forms the basis of Jewish observance and was later codified into the *Mishnah*, the *Gemara* and much later into the *Shulchan Aruch*, the Code of Jewish Law. The *Mishnah* is the first redaction of the Oral Law. It was organized and edited by Rabbi Yehudah HaNasi, the head of the Jewish community, around the year 200 C.E.

blood, it also must be one of five specific colors — either black or four specific shades of red. Although we assume that we know to which type of black the *Mishnah* is referring, the knowledge as to which shades of red are *tahor*, spiritu–ally pure, and which are *tamei*, spiritually impure, was lost by the time of the writing of the *Gemara*, approximately 1,700 years ago.[10] It is generally understood that this *mesorah*, or "tradition," was lost because of the spiritual decline of the Jewish people.[11]

Hence, since the time that the *mesorah* was lost, any shade of red is treated as *niddah* blood (if the other conditions are met). However, different traditions exist for deciding whether shades of color similar to red — such as brown, gold and pink — are also considered *niddah* colors or not.

Colors: Which Are Niddah?

Colors can look quite different when viewed in various types of light. For example, incandescent lighting can make colors appear darker than they actually are. Eyeglasses, particularly those with an anti-scratch coating, can alter a color's appearance.

For a color to be interpreted correctly, it must be viewed in indirect natural daylight or, if unavailable, flourescent light. In addition, the fabric on which the color is found should be put on top of something white for accurate viewing.

Colors also fade over time. If you have a question about a color, try to get it resolved within two days. (See the section below, *Asking Questions About Colors*.)

Non-Niddah Colors

Non-*niddah* colors are white, off-white, tan, beige, clear, light yellow, light grey, light blue and light green.[12] (A blue or green discharge, however, may indicate an infection. If you see these colors, consult your doctor.)

---

[10] See *Niddah* 20b, where the *Amorayim* (the rabbis of the time of the writing of the *Gemara*) state that they no longer had the expertise to discern between *tamei* and *tahor* blood.

[11] *Niddah* 20b ; Tur *Yoreh Deah* 188.

[12] *Yoreh Deah* 188:1.

Niddah Colors

Niddah colors are red, red-brown and black.[13] It should be noted that if you see red blood (especially bright red) at a time when you are not expecting your period — or your period just doesn't seem to end — the blood may be coming from some type of wound. In this case, it may be best to first consult a niddah nurse (an observant woman — usually a nurse or midwife — who has been specially trained to find out the source of the bleeding). If a niddah nurse is unavailable in your community, choose a doctor or midwife that can understand these types of problems.[14]

Questionable Colors

Colors which may or may not be indicative of niddah include orange, brown,[15] dark yellow, gold, pink,[16] darker shades of blue and green, purple and grey.[17] According to the tradition of many authorities in Jewish law, these colors themselves are not indicative of niddah blood. It is only when they have red mixed into them that they are considered niddah colors. Other authorities rule differently. If you see a questionable color, it is important to consult an expert in this area of Jewish law. (See below Asking Questions About Colors.)

Asking Questions About Colors

Getting answers to questions about matters of niddah can be arranged with

---

13   Yoreh Deah 188:1.
14   For example, a small wound on the outside of the cervix or in the wall of the vagina (both common problems) can bleed for many days, especially if irritated by a foreign object such as a bedikah cloth, tampon or the like. This would not be niddah blood, since it results from a wound; however, outside verification is almost always needed to differentiate between niddah blood and blood from a wound. Note: If the abnormal blood is determined to be niddah, it can be an indicator of a hormonal problem or even a serious illness (which, when attended to in its early stages, can usually be arrested).
15   A discharge of a non-niddah brown color is often an indication of dehydration.
16   Many authorities rule that light pink is not a niddah color. In addition, it should be noted that pink often indicates a wound that is healing or a yeast infection.
17   Since these colors may have black in them.

the utmost privacy and dignity. For help in matters of procedure, ask a knowledgeable, observant woman in your community.

A *halachic* authority well-versed in the laws of *niddah* will be able to discern whether the color you are seeing is a *niddah* color or not. In addition, for a woman having a medical problem, many authorities are able to diagnose quite accurately the nature of the problem.

Asking questions can save days, sometimes weeks, of unnecessary separation between a husband and wife, as well as much needless anxiety. Asking questions about colors can also make the difference between being able to conceive a child or not.

It is important to keep a *Torah* perspective on asking questions about colors. Our tradition tells us there is nothing in the physical world too mundane to be sanctified. The *Gemara* relates that King David, who was the greatest *halachic* authority of his time, spent countless hours examining different blood stains to determine if they were *tahor* (spiritually "pure"), or *tamei* (spiritually "impure").[18] We sanctify ourselves and thus join in a partnership with the Almighty by doing His will. To ask a question about these matters is no cause for embarrassment; rather, it's doing the will of our Creator.

2. The Blood Did Not Come From a Wound

Blood originating from a wound in the tissue — whether cervical, uterine or vaginal — does not make a woman *niddah*.[19]

If you notice blood and you aren't expecting your period, or your period just doesn't seem to end, it may be due to a wound in the tissue. In this case, it's best to first consult a *niddah* nurse. If a *niddah* nurse is unavailable is your community, consult a doctor or midwife that has expertise in these types of problems.

In some instances, it is possible to say with certainty that blood is coming from a wound; other cases are not so clear cut, which makes them more compli-

---

[18] *Brachos* 4a.
[19] *Niddah* 16a.

cated. If, after being checked, your practitioner finds a wound but cannot determine with certainty that the blood is solely coming from the wound, note the circumstances and consult your *halachic* authority.

If you notice unexpected bleeding, but it stops before you can arrange with a practitioner to be checked, you should still be checked professionally. Ask your practitioner the following questions, then consult your *halachic* authority to determine whether or not you are *niddah*:[20]

♦ Can it be determined that there is an irritation, infection or condition above the cervix (that is, in the cervical canal or the uterus)? Can it be determined with *certainty* that this condition is causing bleeding or might be causing bleeding?

♦ Can it be determined that there is an irritation or infection on the outside of the cervix or in the vaginal canal— such as a laceration, ulceration, inflammation, etc. — that *normally* causes bleeding?

Bleeding from a regular internal exam or from a pap smear does not make a woman *niddah*; neither does bleeding from irritation following a cervical biopsy. In both of these cases, the blood would have had to have originated from the irritation, since neither of these procedures opens the womb. If you are unsure what the doctor is doing, ask so that you will have the information you need to consult with a *halachic* expert later.

In the rare event that a woman needs a procedure where an instrument is inserted through the cervix, she may or may not become *niddah*, depending on the diameter of the instrument,[21] even if no blood was found.[22] If you are in need of such a procedure,

---

[20] *Niddah* 58b; *Yoreh Deah* 190:18.

[21] Most authorities rule that the instrument must be larger than the width of a finger to render a woman *niddah* (*Igros Moshe Yoreh Deah* 1:89). However, *Badei HaShulchan* 194:31 rules that the minimum dimension is fifteen millimeters.

[22] This is due to the principle, "There is no opening of the womb without blood," even if the blood is not seen (*Ohalos* 7:4, as understood by Responsum *Shu't Noda BiYehudah* Vol. 2 *Yoreh*

it is best to find out all the necessary information beforehand from your doctor and then consult a *halachic* authority. If you know in advance that the procedure will make you *niddah*, you can plan your doctor's visit to coincide with the end of your period.

3. A Hargashah Was Experienced

The *Gemara* relates that in *Talmudic* times a woman would actually feel her cervix opening to allow the blood of menstruation to leave.[23] This sensation is called *hargashah* and, in fact, was a sensation so evident that if a woman was sleeping when her period started, this sensation was strong enough to awaken her.

Today, we have lost the sensitivity to feel this change in our bodies, even though this is precisely what happens physiologically. However, even though we do not feel *hargashah*, if we have reason to believe that a woman experienced it (by the simple fact that her period began), we can say that she is truly *niddah*, according to *Torah* law.[24]

It is instructive to note a number of cases where the *Gemara* talks about different ways the sensation of *hargashah* can happen and a woman might not feel it. Each of these cases offers important insights for all women keeping the laws of *niddah*.

- ♦ There are times when a woman checks herself internally for the presence of blood using a special cloth (called a *bedikah* cloth). If there was a sensation of *hargashah* at the very same time that she was checking herself, it is assumed that she wouldn't have noticed the *hargashah*, since she could easily confuse the sensation of her hargasha with the sensation caused by the cloth.[25] Therefore, if blood is found on a cloth that was used for an internal check, no matter how small a speck, the woman is considered *niddah*

Deah 120). This principle applies when the womb has been opened because something entered or exited. A dilated or open cervix does not, in itself, render a woman *niddah*.

23   *Niddah* 3a.

24   *Aruch HaShulchan* 183:61; *Shiurei Shevet HaLevi* 190:1:2.

25   *Niddah* 57b.

by *Torah* law (barring certain exceptional circumstances,
such as when she has a wound that is bleeding).[26]

Since there is no requirement that a woman check herself when the *halachah*
does not mandate it,[27] if she has any question whether she must check herself,
she should first consult an authority on Jewish law before before making any
internal check. Many times, what looks like blood can be explained for a number
of reasons that are not *niddah* according to Jewish law (as will be discussed below). But once a red stain is found on a *bedikah* cloth, the situation becomes more
complicated.

- ✦ In a similar case, the *Gemara* assumes that a woman would
  not feel the sensation of *hargashah* if it happened while she
  was passing urine.[28]

Therefore, if a woman finds blood immediately following urination she may
be *niddah*. However, in this situation Jewish law makes the following distinc-
tions: If the blood is in the urine itself, the woman is not considered *niddah*. She is
also not *niddah* if she felt pain when she was urinating and immediately afterwards she found blood. (These are classic symptoms of a urinary tract infection;
if you experience these symptoms, see a doctor.) But if she finds blood immediately after urination without pain (not in the urine), it is likely that she is *niddah*,
and she should consult a *halachic* authority.[29]

Blood Found on Toilet Paper

The most common question that arises from the above case is, what if she
finds what looks like blood on toilet paper? This is actually a complex question

---

[26] *Yoreh Deah* 190:33. See also, *Sidrei Taharah* 183:2; *Chavos Daas* 183:2; *Pischei Teshuvah* 183:1.
[27] Indeed, many *halachic* authorities discourage this (see *Posayach Shaar* 8:30 and Rabbi Forst,
      Vol. 1 pg. 175 and 183); however, a minority of authorities requires a woman to make a *bedikah*
      when she discovers a stain, (*kesem*). See *Shiurei Shevet HaLevi* 190:5:1.
[28] *Niddah* 57b.
[29] *Yoreh Deah* 191.

in Jewish law. Because of these complex issues, many authorities simply recommend not looking at toilet paper, since it is not required by *halachah*.[30]

To some women, this may sound like "cheating." So, why does *halachah* tell us to do this? First, Jewish law is the first to urge us not to go out of our way to become *niddah*, especially when there is no reason to suspect anything wrong. Second, most likely, whatever you find is probably not *niddah* blood.[31] Thus, it is very possible that a woman can end up separated from her husband unnecessarily.[32]

If a woman wants to look at toilet paper without unnecessarily becoming *niddah*, she should wait a few moments before using the toilet paper. Then, according to the majority of *halachic* authorities,[33] if she finds what looks like blood on the toilet paper, it is not considered to have emanated from an undetected *hargashah* that happened when she passed urine (and therefore, in most cases, will not make her *niddah*). For more details on finding a stain on toilet paper, see the section below, *Special Circumstances: Finding a Stain When Not Niddah*.

Feeling a Flow While Not Niddah

Since most women experience some sort of sensation of flow or moving fluid during their cycle, particularly at times they are not expecting their period, e.g., during ovulation, is a woman required to do a *bedikah* every time she feels such a sensation? The answer is no, once the following procedure has been completed:

---

[30] See *Posayach Shaar* 8:30.

[31] Since in our times, we don't even know the exact colors of red that are truly indicative of *niddah*.

[32] Interestingly, we have a similar *halachah* when checking eggs for blood. We check raw eggs because we know the color of blood in an egg that is raw. We don't check hard-boiled eggs because we don't know what the color of blood looks like once the egg is cooked. Therefore, if we would find something suspicious in a hard-boiled egg, we would be apt to throw it out. Because the egg is most likely good, this would be a violation of ba'al tashchis, the prohibition not to waste food. Therefore, Jewish law holds that we don't check hard-boiled eggs for blood (as heard from Rav Yitzchak Berkovits).

[33] *Igros Moshe Yoreh Deah* IV:17. The time lag allows the stain in question to fall under the laws of a stain (*kesem*).

The first three times you feel this type of sensation at a time you are not expecting your period, check yourself with a *bedikah* cloth. If, after three consecutive times, you found that everything is fine, then you are not obligated to check yourself again when you feel this sensation. You can henceforth always assume this sensation is not indicative of *niddah* for you.[34] (This is in contrast to feeling a sensation of a flow at a time when you are expecting your period, when this sensation can indicate that your period has indeed begun.)

Special Circumstances: Finding a Stain While Not Niddah

What happens if you are not expecting your period and had no awareness of any flow of blood, yet nevertheless find a *niddah*-colored stain, *kesem*, on your undergarments, sheets, body, etc.? A stain is different from other types of bleeding in that it is not accompanied by any feeling of flow having left the body. This type of stain is a question of rabbinic law, since it does not meet the *Torah* requirements for *niddah*.

Becoming Niddah Through Staining

A woman can become *niddah* from finding such a stain, but only if a specific set of conditions are met, which we will discuss below. Since this type of *niddah* was instituted by rabbinic law,[35] it is important to keep in mind that just as our Sages instituted these laws, they also defined their paramenters, which, as we shall see, are limited to specific situations. If your circumstance is not included within these parameters, you do not become *niddah* through finding a stain.

To become *niddah* by finding a stain, all of the following three conditions must be met:[36]

1. The size of the *niddah*-colored stain must be larger than a *gris*, which is about

---

[34] *Shu't Divrei Chayim* 1:34; *Shu't Maharsham* 1:188; *Shiurei Shevet HaLevi* 190:1:11.
[35] These laws were based on the laws of ritual purity concerning the *Beis HaMikdash*.
[36] *Yoreh Deah* 190.

19 millimeters in diameter or slightly larger than a U.S. dime or an Israeli one shekel coin. If there is more than one *niddah*-colored stain, you need to be concerned only if one of the stains is larger than a *gris*. If there are a number of *niddah*-colored stains, each less than a *gris*, their combined size is measured only if they are connected.[37] Similarly, if the *niddah*-colored stains are part of a non-*niddah*-colored stain, the size of the *niddah*-colored stains are combined only if they are connected.[38]

2. The object on which the stain is found must be white;

3. The object on which the stain is found must be capable of absorbing spiritual impurity, what is known in Hebrew as being able to *mekabel tumah*. Anything that is connected to the ground (for example, a toilet seat or a bathtub) does not absorb spiritual impurity, but anything that once originated in the ground and then made into a "utensil" (roughly defined as something useful in a permanent way) does.[39] Most authorities agree that all fabrics, whether cotton or synthetic, are *mekabel tumah*. Many authorities rule that toilet paper cannot *mekabel tumah*, since it is not considered to be a "utensil" by *halachah* (since it is made to be discarded).[40] Therefore, as long as you waited a few moments before using the toilet paper (as we discussed above), finding a stain on toilet paper cannot make you *niddah*.

In general, a stain on the body can only render a woman *niddah* if it is found on parts of the body onto which the blood could have fallen if it had emanated from her uterus.[41]

Most importantly, as in all areas of Jewish life, do not hesitate to consult a

---

[37] Glosses of Rabbi Akiva Eiger on *Yoreh Deah* 190:10 (quoting *Me'il Tzedakah*) and *Pischei Teshuvah* 190:20.

[38] Ibid.

[39] *Pischei Teshuvah* 190:18.

[40] Ruling the same way, but using a slightly different line of reasoning, Rav Moshe Feinstein (*Igros Moshe Yoreh Deah* IV:17) rules that once toilet paper is used, it becomes garbage and thus cannot *mekabel tumah*.

[41] These areas are detailed in the *Shulchan Aruch*; see *Taz* 190:37.

halachic authority if you find a questionable stain. Our Sages who established these laws also established their parameters. A stain that might seem to you to indicate that you are *niddah* may, in reality, be outside these established parameters.[42]

Equally important, if you do find a stain, consult a *halachic* authority before checking yourself with a *bedikah* cloth.[43] As we discussed above, even if it is very unlikely that the stain you have found is *niddah* blood, once the tiniest speck of blood has been found on a *bedikah* cloth, it becomes highly problematic and can make you *niddah*.

---

[42] It is evident that our Sages did not intend that a woman will easily become *niddah* through discovering a stain — even going so far as to attribute a stain on a woman's underwear to a paper cut on her finger or to a trip to the butcher. See *Yoreh Deah* 190:18, based on *Niddah* 58b.

[43] See *Posayach Shaar* 8:30 and Rabbi Forst, Vol. 1 pg. 175 and 183.

CHAPTER 4

♦

The Laws of Separation

The laws prescribing how a husband and wife may relate to each other while she is *niddah* — and they are separate — are called the *harchakos*, literally "distancings."

Although some of these laws may at first seem awkward to follow, with time you will find that they serve to forge new levels of intimate awareness between you and your husband. Refraining from certain acts that we normally perceive as mundane elevates them into the realm of the precious. When you are not *niddah*, even the simplest exchange between you and your husband — like passing the house keys from one to the other — can become an act of intimacy and a means of connection, precisely because this was denied to you for almost half the month.

Judaism teaches that elevating the level of intimacy between a husband and wife is one of the highest forms of holiness in this world.[1] Although it may take time to reorient yourself to this way of thinking, it is a beautiful thing to be able to take any action we do in the physical world and elevate it to the realm of holiness.

---

[1]   Our Sages liken marital intimacy to peace in the home (*Shabbos* 152) and remark that this type of peace is "great" (*Chullin* 141a). Increasing the level of intimacy, love and desire between husband and wife also positively affects the children they will bear together (*Sefer Chassidim* 362).

Affectionate Contact

While a woman is *niddah*, affectionate contact between her and her husband is forbidden by the *Torah*, as it states, "Do not come near a woman who is *niddah*."[2]

This is an extremely serious prohibition. Were a couple to intentionally have marital relations while the wife is *niddah*, they would incur the punishment of *karais*, one of the more severe punishments (spiritual consequences) mentioned in the *Torah*.[3] Intimate contact during this time is also considered one of the forbidden "sexual" acts, called *arayos*, for which a Jewish person must give up his life rather than commit.[4]

Lesser forms of affectionate contact are also forbidden by the *Torah* while the wife is *niddah*.[5]

However, if either the husband's or the wife's life were in danger, they may touch each other in order to save each others' lives.[6]

---

[2] *Vayikra* 18:19.

[3] Rambam (*Hilchos Teshuvah* 8:1) explains *karais* to be the termination of the soul. *Sifra* (to *Vayikra* 23:28) describes *karais* as "destruction" without specifying. Ramban (*Shaar HaGmul*, Ch. 6) interprets *Sifra* to mean "cut off from *Gan Eden* ("Paradise")". *Tosafos* to *Yevamos* 2a s.v. *Eishes* explains that the punishment for this sin (prohibited sexual relationships) is premature death and death of one's children in one's lifetime.

[4] There is a dispute between Rambam and Ramban. Rambam (*Hilchos Issurei Bi'ah* 21:1) considers any "intimate contact" — even hugging and kissing — to be a sin for which one is required to give up his life. Ramban disagrees. See also *Beis Yosef* and *Shach* to *Yoreh Deah*, end of Ch. 195.

[5] Although these other forms of affectionate contact incur a consequence less than *karais*.

[6] Although the *Shulchan Aruch* (*Yoreh Deah* 195:17) prohibits any physical contact between husband and wife while the wife is *niddah*, the accepted practice for both *Ashkenazim* and *Sefardim* alike is to follow the opinion of Rama, who permits (non-affectionate) physical contact to save a life or for medical reasons under extenuating circumstances (195:16,17). However, Rav Ovadiah Yosef permits this type of contact only to save a life or if the husband is ill (*Taharas HaBayis* 12:46).

Also (as heard from Rav Yitzchak Berkovits), if no one else is around, a husband is allowed to touch his wife to calm her if she truly needs this help during childbirth (even at a point when she has already become *niddah*), since we never take chances with childbirth. It is understood that what often makes childbirth dangerous is the level of tension that a woman feels. However, a husband in this situation must be extremely careful that his touch is calming and not affectionate. Even if a woman has the option of taking medication (which

Yichud: Being Alone Together

According to *halachah*, a man and woman who are not married may not be secluded together, that is, to be in a place inaccessible to others.[7] No matter what they are doing, the *Torah* considers such a seclusion itself as inappropriate.[8] This prohibition, which is known as *yichud*, does not apply to a husband and wife while the wife is *niddah*. Our Sages explain that *yichud* is permitted during this time, because both the husband and wife are aware that this is a temporary separation, and they will be together again.[9] (Other exceptions where *yichud* is generally allowed include *yichud* between fathers and daughters, mothers and sons, grandparents and grandchildren, and brothers and sisters.[10])

Looking at One Another

Jewish law also prohibits a man from staring — for the purpose of deriving pleasure — at an *ervah*, a person who, by *Torah* law, is sexually prohibited to him.[11]

---

would calm her and negate the need for her husband to touch her), she is not obligated by *halachah* to do so. (See also Rama, *Yoreh Deah* 195:17.) Moreover, the long-term effects of these drugs on the mother and the baby are unknown (as heard from Rav Yitzchak Berkovits). Of course, we try never to put ourselves in such a situation and always endeavor to have other assistance around since it is very difficult to distinguish between a calming touch and an affectionate one.

7 *Kiddushin* 80b.

8 Most *rishonim* agree that *yichud* is a *Torah* prohibition (*Kiddushin* 80b, inferred from *Devarim* 13:7.

9 *Tosafos* to *Sotah* 7a and to *Sanhedrin* 37a.

10 *Yichud* between fathers and daughters and sons and mothers is permitted by *Kiddushin* 80b; *yichud* between grandfathers and granddaughters is disputed by commentaries to *Shulchan Aruch*; *Bach Even HaEzer* 21 and *Chelkas Mechokek* 21:10 permit it, while *Beis Shmuel* and others forbid it. *Yichud* between grandmothers and grandsons is permitted by Tur *Yoreh Deah* 362. *Kiddushin* 81b states that *yichud* between brothers and sisters is permitted but implies that (as adults) they are not permitted to dwell together (as pointed out by Rashi). "Dwell together" implies on a permanent basis, which, according to *halachah* is more than 30 days (*Dvar Halachah* 2:4, quoting *Imrei Yosher*).

11 *Shabbos* 64b, Rambam, *Hilchos Issurei Bi'ah* 21:2, *Even HaEzer* 21:1 This prohibition is also derived from the laws of *arayos*.

The *Gemara* says that the one exception to this rule is a husband and wife while the wife is *niddah*,[12] reasoning (as in the case of *yichud* above) that even though the couple is prohibited to one another, they will not be so forever.

However, while his wife is *niddah*, *halachah* forbids a husband from seeing any part of his wife that is "normally covered."[13] "Normally covered" means what you usually cover when in your house with your husband. That is, anything your husband doesn't see frequently, he shouldn't see when you are *niddah*.[14]

For example, if you normally cover your hair in your house around your husband, even though he occasionally sees it uncovered, you should cover your hair in front of him while *niddah*.[15]

If the two of you need to dress in the same room, it is fine for him to simply turn around while you change; he doesn't have to leave the room.[16]

Singing

According to *halachah*, a woman's singing voice — known as *kol ishah* — is considered seductive. Therefore, generally speaking, a woman is forbidden to sing in front of a man, and a man is forbidden to listen to a woman sing.[17] While this

---

[12] *Nedarim* 20a.

[13] Ibid.

[14] *Igros Moshe Yoreh Deah* II:75. Rav Moshe Feinstein rules that one should endeavor to be more stringent in all these laws, unless doing so will create *shalom bayis* problems.

[15] If your husband is used to seeing your hair uncovered in the house, you don't have to cover it in front of him while *niddah*. However, Rav Moshe says that one should endeavor to be more stringent in all these laws, unless doing so will create *shalom bayis* problems. Ibid.

[16] Even if your husband is used to seeing you change clothes, it is likely that most of the time you walk around the house dressed, i.e. "normally covered." Therefore, he should not see you change your clothes while *niddah* (Ibid). There is no prohibition against a wife seeing her husband change clothes or seeing any part of his body while *niddah*. The reason for this difference, and similar other differences in the *harchakos*, is that the main purpose of these laws is to remind the man that his wife is *niddah*. The *Gemara* comments (*Kesubos* 64b) that, in general, it is harder for men to control themselves than it is for women and, therefore, it is the men who need the reminders.

[17] The laws of *kol ishah* are derived from the laws of *arayos*, which govern forbidden sexual relationships (*Brachos* 24a). As in the case of *yichud*, *kol ishah* does not apply between fathers and daughters, mothers and sons, brothers and sisters, and grandparents and grandchildren.

prohibition does not apply to a married couple when the wife is not *niddah*, most *halachic* authorities say that when the wife is *niddah*, she may not sing in front of her husband.[18]

Special Prohibitions

In addition to the laws described above, there are a number of special *harchakos* instituted by our Sages that apply to husband and wife while she is *niddah*.[19] There are two opinions as to why these additional laws were instituted:

The first opinion is that of Rashi,[20] who reasons that since *yichud* is permitted between husband and wife (that is, they are allowed to be completely alone together while she is *niddah*), these extra laws serve to remind the couple to keep a certain distance from one another.

The second opinion, that of the Vilna Gaon, states that these extra laws are necessary because of the nature of the relationship between husband and wife. Certain acts take on intimate meaning between a married couple, but they are insignificant between strangers.[21]

Passing Objects

Among these special *harkachos* is a prohibition of passing or handing objects directly to one other during *niddah*. This prohibition is an extension of the laws

---

[18] Although *Pischei Teshuvah* 195:10, *Lechem VeSimlah* 195:20 and *Kitzur Shulchan Aruch* 153:10 prohibit, others permit, including Rav Ovadiah Yosef in *Taharas HaBayis* 12:29, who quotes several (*Ashkenazi*) sources (including *To'afos Re'eim* 26:130) that permit and rules this way also. Their basis for permitting is because the wife's singing is not exposing her husband to *ervah*. Whereas it is prohibited for other men to hear a woman sing because of temptation, hearing one's own wife sing is more comparable to the prohibition of *yichud*, which does not apply between a married couple (because they know that their physical separation is only temporary). It should also be noted that some authorities also permit a woman to sing in the presence of men to calm her children down. (*Taharas HaBayis* 12:29.) Of course, if men are present and a woman needs to sing to calm her children, it is proper to do this in the least obtrusive way.

[19] *Yoreh Deah* 195.

[20] *Shabbos* 11a.

[21] Gra to *Yoreh Deah* 195:8.

of touching. This means that during *niddah*, while handing an object to your husband, you first will need to put the object down, so he can then pick it up. Included in this law is the prohibition of carrying the same object together, even if it is very heavy.[22] In addition, a couple is not allowed to throw objects directly to one another. However, throwing an object up in the air so your spouse can catch it is permitted, since the object is not thrown directly.[23]

A couple is also not allowed to touch one another through clothing or touch the other's clothing while it is being worn.[24]

Handing Small Children and Babies to One Another

Many questions arise regarding the practical application of the above *halachah* in regards to small children and babies. The following is a general synopsis of these laws:

If a child is able to walk by himself or herself, both parents are allowed to hold one of the child's hands at the same time while walking together. Most contemporary *halachic* authorities prohibit one spouse from putting a baby down on the other spouse's lap as well as picking up a baby from the other's lap (unless, in the latter case, the child is reaching for the other parent).[25] Most authorities also prohibit lifting a baby's stroller together, even in times of difficulty.[26]

Although not passing directly to your spouse or carrying an item together can, at times, be awkward, most couples find creative ways to accomplish these things. However, even in awkward situations, passing directly is not allowed.[27]

---

[22] Rav Moshe Feinstein (*Igros Moshe Yoreh Deah* 2:75) prohibits, Rav Ovadiah Yosef permits (*Taharas HaBayis* 2:89) as do others (*Shu't Tzitz Eliezer* 12:58).

[23] *Birkei Yosef* 195:6.

[24] *Pischei Teshuvah* 195:3.

[25] *Pischei Teshuvah* 195:3; *Badei HaShulchan* and *Shiurei Shevet HaLevi* ad loc.

[26] *Igros Moshe Yoreh Deah* 2:75 says it is appropriate to be stringent on this matter. Also see *Sugah BaShoshanim* 21:8 and *Badei HaShulchan* 195:26. Others (*Chut Shani* 195:3[4], *Shu't Tzitz Eliezer* 12:58) permit lifting a stroller together in a time of difficulty. These sources note that the husband and wife must lift the stroller from different sides.

[27] *Chayei Adam* 130; *Igros Moshe Yoreh Deah* 2:77; *Badei HaShulchan* 195:22.

It is worth noting that being *niddah* should not and need not be a source of embarrassment.[28]

Eating Together

In general, we will see that the basis for the prohibitions regarding eating together remind a couple not to eat in ways that are intimate.

Individual Portions

An individual plate or portion of food may not be shared (meaning, eaten at the same time) by the husband and wife while the wife is *niddah*. This prohibition also includes sharing an item of food made for an individual, like a roll or a small can of soda, even if it is sliced or portioned out, since sharing a food like this is a form of intimacy between husband and wife.[29] (However, if you need to share an individual item of food, for example, you only have one individual roll for the third meal of *Shabbos*, one spouse should eat his or her portion and the other should eat the rest according to the laws of leftovers, which are discussed below.)

Eating food that is taken from a common bowl, or eating food served in a form that is clearly made for a number of people (like a cake that is sliced into individual pieces) is fine. Eating this way, "family style," is not considered intimate; it is a normal way of eating with strangers or guests. The same *halachah* applies to a large bag of popcorn or the like. However, when partaking from common food, each spouse must first place the food on his or her own plate (or napkin) before eating it. Neither should eat directly from the serving bowl, platter, bag, etc.

Leftovers

A wife may eat her husband's leftovers directly (i.e., from his plate), but a husband may only eat his wife's leftovers indirectly. How does this work practically? In general, for your husband to finish your food, it must first be put on

---

[28] See *Igros Moshe Yoreh Deah* 2:77; *Badei HaShulchan* 195:22. See also *Kesubos* 72a which implies that a woman wore certain distinctive outer garments when she was *niddah*.

[29] *Igros Moshe Yoreh Deah* 1:92.

another plate, unless you have left the room, or he was unaware that it was your food.

What if the leftovers are of the type of food that a stranger wouldn't eat, for example, an apple from which you've taken a bite or any other partially eaten piece of food? For a husband to finish this type of leftovers from his wife, the bitten part needs to be cut off and the rest put on a different plate, whether his wife is present or not. It now becomes the type of food a stranger would eat.

Eating at the Table Together

When the wife is *niddah* and eating with her husband, they must have something on the table or between their plates to remind them to keep a certain distance from each other. For example, you may eat on placemats if you don't do so normally or place an object on the table between you and your husband that obviously doesn't belong there or isn't needed for the meal.

Many authorities hold that this requirement is only necessary when the two of you are eating alone, but that it is not necessary when others are present. If you follow the stricter opinion and put a reminder on the table when others are present, the reminder does not have to be obvious.

Serving Food and Drinks

The *Gemara* states that one of the things a woman may not do for her husband while she is *niddah* is *mezeigas ha-cos*.[30] We know that the Hebrew word *cos* means cup, but we are not so sure of the meaning of *mezeigas*.

The opinion which is followed today interprets this phrase to mean that a wife is prohibited from serving any food or drink to her husband directly while *niddah*.[31]

What does it mean not to serve your husband directly? The *Gemara* states that not serving directly means serving in an abnormal way.[32] For example, putting

---

[30] *Kesubos* 61a.
[31] *Shach Yoreh Deah* 195:13. The more lenient opinion interprets this phrase to mean that a wife may not mix wine and water for her husband and serve it to him.
[32] *Kesubos* 61a.

his food or drink down where it doesn't belong, i.e., off to the side so that he has to pull it toward himself, or serving him using your left hand if you are right-handed. If he is not present, you may put his food or drink directly in front of his place.

Just as it is prohibited for a wife to serve her husband directly while she is *niddah*, since it may cause him to think about her intimately,[33] it is equally prohib-ited for a husband to serve his wife food or drink directly.

The source for this *halachah* is the *rishonim*, who considered it an intimate act for a husband to send a cup of wine to his wife, even through a third party.[34] This idea is derived from the story about the *Amora* Shmuel (Samuel, the scholar) and his wife. Shmuel would often send a cup of wine to his wife. If she refused to accept it, he would know that she had become *niddah* (her way of conveying a private message in a public place).[35]

From this story, it is reasoned that if it is considered romantic for a man to send his wife a cup of wine (i.e., designate a cup of wine for her), then certainly it must be romantic to serve her wine directly. The prevailing custom became to extend this prohibition to the direct serving of all food and drinks (from hus-band to wife) while the wife is *niddah*.

Kiddush on Shabbos

If a husband cannot send or designate a cup of wine for his wife while she is *niddah*, the question arises as to how he should serve her *kiddush* wine on *Shabbos*. Many discreet options exist from which the couple can choose, according to their preference.

If it is your custom to drink directly from your husband's *kiddush* cup, then after making the blessing and drinking the wine, your husband can simply put the cup down in front of himself, and you can pick it up and drink from it (and distribute it to your guests, if present). Similarly, after making the blessing, drink-

---

[33] Rashi to *Kesubos* 61a.

[34] The *rishonim* base this on a *halachic Midrash* in *Mesechta Kallah*.

[35] Ibid.

ing the wine and putting the cup down in front of himself, a guest or child can hand you your husband's cup.

If it is your husband's custom to pour wine out of the *kiddush* cup (to give to others), you may follow the same procedures as above, since either way, your husband hasn't sent the cup to you.[36]

Alternatively, your husband can fill small cups for everyone present. If the cups are together on a tray, he can initially pass the tray to a guest or child close to him, or you can pass the tray around. This way, everyone chooses their own cup, and none has been designated. Similarly, if the little cups aren't on a tray, you can distribute the cups and choose one for yourself.

It's a good idea to decide which way works for you and your husband, and then serve it this way *niddah* or not. This way, you never run into an awkward situation if guests are present, and one of you forgets about these prohibitions.

Sleeping on Separate Beds

During *niddah*, a husband and wife must sleep on separate beds that do not touch each other.[37] They also may not lay down, even fully clothed in the same bed, even if there are separate matresses.[38]

In addition, this *halachah* was extended to prohibit the husband from sitting on his wife's bed while she is *niddah*, even if she is not present, unless she is out of town. A wife, however, is allowed to sit on her husband's bed while she is *niddah*, even if he is in the room. She is also allowed to lie down on his bed, but only when he is not present.[39]

How far the beds should be apart is a matter of opinion. According to Rama, the beds should simply not touch.[40] Others say that the beds should be far enough

---

[36]   You are merely drinking his leftovers.
[37]   Rama, *Yoreh Deah* 195:6.
[38]   Ibid.
[39]   This prohibition is found in *Shabbos* 13a and its extension in *Tur* and *Shulchan Aruch Yoreh Deah* 195.
[40]   Rama, *Yoreh Deah* 195:6.

apart so that their blankets don't touch;[41] still others say that the beds should be far enough apart that if either spouse were to reach his or her arm out in the middle of the night, it wouldn't touch the other spouse.[42] There is no opinion that requires an object (such as a night table) to be placed between the beds.

Questions often arise about separate beds that share a common headboard. If the headboard is not attached to the beds (for example, it is attached to the wall), it is fine. If not, our *halachic* authorities agree that while one shouldn't buy furniture like this in the first place, if you already have beds with this design, you are allowed to use them while *niddah*.[43]

Exchanging Beds

If a husband and wife need to exchange beds while *niddah* — for example, winter comes and one of you is too cold near a window — the physical location of the beds may be changed, even if the husband's bed is now in the place where his wife's once was (and vice-versa).[44] However, a couple is not allowed to simply sleep in each other's beds, as we discussed above (with the exception that a wife is allowed to lie down on her husband's bed when he is not present). While you are not *niddah*, you may sleep in each other's bed (or switch mattresses) and then make the change permanent.[45]

Making the Beds

The *Gemara* states that while a wife is *niddah*, she may not "straighten her husband's bed in front of him."[46] Here, the *Gemara* is referring to personal gestures (as opposed to toil) specifically, a wife preparing her husband's bed for him before sleep while he is watching, such as fluffing up his pillow and the like.[47] How-

---

41 *Darchei Teshuvah* 33.
42 *Taharas Yisroel* 195:27.
43 See *Shiurei Sheivet HaLevi* 195:6(2).
44 *Shiurei Shevet HaLevi* 195:5:3; *Sugah BaShoshanim* 13:28.
45 Ibid.
46 *Kesubos* 61a.
47 *Yoreh Deah* 195:11.

ever, it has become the accepted custom to extend this *halachah* to include a wife not making or changing her husband's bed while he is watching.[48]

There is no prohibition against a husband making his wife's bed while she is *niddah*, even though it is not generally done. Most likely, this practice comes from the time when servants made all the beds. Because of this, the *Gemara* mentions that a wife who has servants to do all her domestic work should nevertheless do something personal for her husband, like make his bed.[49]

Sitting Together

While *niddah*, a husband and wife may not sit on an object at the same time that is not connected to the ground and is not stiff, unless there is a person (even a baby) or an object between them.[50] An example of this type of furniture is a soft couch with only one cushion. This is because one can readily feel the other's body weight and movement on such a piece of furniture. You may sit at the same time on a couch if it is firm. However, if the couch is soft you may sit on it together (without an object or person between you) only if it is attached to the floor or if it has separate cushions.[51]

What about sitting in cars and buses together?

Today, many cars and buses have separate seats, which pose no problems. However, if you want to sit together on a soft seat that only has one cushion in a car or bus, you may do so if you have either a person or an object between you and your husband.[52]

Pleasure Rides and Walks

Another one of the special *harchakos* prohibits husband and wife from going on pleasure rides together while sitting next to each other during *niddah*.[53] A

---

[48] See *Lechem VeSimlah* 195:25.
[49] *Kesubos* 61a.
[50] Rama, *Yoreh Deah* 195:5.
[51] Ibid.
[52] As inferred from the previous sources.
[53] Rama, *Yoreh Deah* 195:5. However, many authorities do allow this type of travel. *Igros Moshe*

"pleasure ride," in this case, is defined as a ride that has no specific destination. Many *halachic* authorities allow this type of travel if the couple is sitting in separate, bucket seats.[54]

You are allowed to travel sitting next to each other if you are travelling to a specific destination, even if the trip is pleasurable. However, you are not allowed to take the scenic route while sitting next to each other to that destination, if it means going out of your way to do so (since the ride itself is pleasurable).

Going on pleasure walks together during the time of *niddah* is permitted, although isolated, romantic spots should be avoided.[55]

Preparing Water

The *Gemara* says that a wife may not "wash the hands, face or feet" of her husband while she is *niddah*.[56] The commentators explain that the *Gemara* is not concerned with a wife touching her husband while doing these things — since we already know this is not allowed while *niddah* — but rather about the intimate aspect of preparing water for the husband to bathe these parts of his body.[57]

This prohibition does not apply if either the water is not prepared in the husband's presence, or if the wife places it before him in an unusual way (for example, with her left hand if she is right-handed).[58]

This prohibition also doesn't apply to a wife preparing water for her husband to wash his hands before morning blessings or before eating bread (unless the couple has turned this into something romantic), or to preparing water for medical reasons (a basin of water for soaking his feet, for example), as none of these activities is considered romantic.

Yoreh Deah 1:92 and 2:83 rules that Rama refers only to a boat, wagon or other lightweight vehicle, but this ruling does not apply to an auto, unless the couple is sitting next to one another closely.

54 See *Chochmas Adam* 116:5. See also *Shiurei Shevet HaLevi* 195:11 s.v. *uvimechonis*.
55 See *Aruch HaShulchan* 195:20.
56 *Kesubos* 61a.
57 *Taz Yoreh Deah* 195:8.
58 *Yoreh Deah* 195:12.

What if your husband's hands are so dirty that he doesn't want to touch the faucet? In this case, you are allowed to turn on the water for him as long as his hands aren't under the faucet at the time.[59]

Similarly, a wife is allowed to turn on the hot water heater so her husband can have hot water for his bath.

The above prohibitions apply equally to a husband preparing water for his wife to wash her hands, face or feet.[60]

Wearing Make-Up and Perfume

A wife is allowed to wear make-up while she is *niddah*;[61] in fact the *Gemara*[62] specifically rules that a wife should appear pleasant for her husband when she is *niddah*. However, perfume may not be worn in a way that one's husband will smell it.[63]

During Illness

A couple may touch in a non-affectionate way while the wife is *niddah* if one of them needs medical or personal care and is too ill to take care of himself or herself and no one else is available. This includes cases where either spouse is bedridden because of severe illness, very weak or in a great amount of pain (although his or her life is not in danger).[64] For example, if a man is in the hospital, and he needs help to go to the bathroom, and no one else is available, his wife can help him.

However, even a wife who is allowed to help her husband during illness may not do things for her husband which are considered intimate, such as preparing

---

[59] This is because the water you prepared — the water that first came out of the faucet — is not the water with which he is washing. In this case, don't stop up the sink beforehand.

[60] *Chochmas Adam* 116:10; *Aruch HaShulchan* 195:14; *Shiurei Sheivet HaLevi* 195:12; *Badei HaShulchan* 195:152.

[61] *Yoreh Deah* 195:9.

[62] *Shabbos* 64b.

[63] *Pischei Teshuvah* 195:1.

[64] Rama, *Yoreh Deah* 195:16, 17. However, note that Rav Ovadiah Yosef permits this type of contact only to save a life or if the husband is ill (*Taharas HaBayis* 12:46).

his bed for him while he is watching or washing him. If his fever is so high that his life is in danger, she may bathe him, sponge him down or do whatever else is necessary.

Special Days When the Harchakos Apply

In addition to the prohibition against marital relations on *Yom Kippur*, all of the *harchakos* apply as well.[65] During *shivah*, marital relations are forbidden and the accepted practice is to refrain from all other forms of affectionate contact, as well .[66] If the wife is not *niddah*, the *harchakos* do not apply.[67]

Some *halachic* authorities treat *Tishah B'Av* according to the laws of *Yom Kippur*, while others treat this day according to the laws of *shivah*.[68]

---

[65] *Orach Chayim* 615:1 and *Mishnah Berurah* ad. loc.

[66] Rama, *Yoreh Deah* 383:1.

[67] *Yoreh Deah* 383.

[68] *Orach Chayim* 554:18 implies that *Tishah B'Av* is more lenient and so rules the *Taz* 615:1. The *Machatzis Hashekel* 554:19 explains that *Yom Kippur* is stricter because the women are dressed up in honor of *Yom Tov*, whereas on *Tishah B'Av* they are dressed in mourning, therefore we need not be as concerned about the *harchakos*. However, *Darchei Moshe* 554:7 (Rama's comments on the Tur, as opposed to his notes on *Shulchan Aruch*) states that maybe the laws of *Tishah B'Av* are the same as *Yom Kippur*; he is quoted there by *Magen Avraham*, who rules that one may be lenient in the daytime. *Mishnah Berurah* 554:37 (essentially quoting the *Darchei Moshe*) implies that one should be strict but does not rule so explicitly.

CHAPTER 5

◆

The Process of Spiritual Purification — a Historical Perspective

Before husband and wife can resume physical contact, the wife must complete a process of spiritual purification that includes:

- ◆ Ascertaining that all (uterine) bleeding has stopped;[1]
- ◆ Counting seven "clean" days; and
- ◆ Immersing in a *mikveh*, "ritual bath."

In this chapter, we will examine the historical and *halachic* reasons behind the first two points and, in the subsequent chapters, their practical application.

Overview

A woman who is *niddah* must first ascertain that all bleeding has stopped. According to normative *halachah*, this is done a minimum of five days after the bleeding began.[2] Once five days have passed and she is certain that the bleeding

---

[1] That is, bleeding from the shedding of the lining of the uterus.

[2] Technically, the *hefsek taharah* can be made before the five days are over; however, the count of the Seven Clean Days may not begin until five days have passed. For example, in a case where a woman has a wound that bleeds at the time when she is obligated to make a *hefsek taharah* (i.e., on the fifth day after her period began), she may make the *hefsek taharah* earlier if

has stopped, she then counts seven consecutive days (free from bleeding), after which she immerses in a *mikveh*. Once she has completed this process, she is no longer *niddah*, and she and her husband may resume their physical relationship.

How these periods of waiting evolved historically and *halachically* is both interesting and instructive. We will first discuss the seven days, commonly referred to as the "Seven Clean Days" (since they are free of blood), which, in turn, will help us understand the first five days.

The Seven Clean Days

The *Torah* mentions two kinds of bleeding which necessitate a husband and wife to separate: [3]

1. Bleeding from normal menstruation, called *niddah*, which lasts seven days or less and

2. Another type of uterine bleeding, called *zavah* bleeding.

Further, the *Torah* states that bleeding from normal menstruation — *niddah* blood — requires that a husband and wife separate for seven days (total). At the end of these seven days, after ascertaining that all the bleeding has stopped, the woman immerses in a *mikveh*, and she is no longer *niddah*.[4]

---

all the bleeding has stopped. She then waits until the five days have passed since the beginning of her period and then counts the Seven Clean Days. In rare circumstances, there are exceptions to this rule, for example, in the case of a woman who bleeds less than five days and ovulates before she can go to the *mikveh*. In this case, a *halachic* authority needs to be consulted to rule if (and how) the five days can be shortened. In addition, a bride before her wedding may begin to count the Seven Clean Days as soon as her period has ended (*Taz Yoreh Deah* 196:7). *Shach Yoreh Deah* 196:20 rules this way only under extenuating circumstances, for example, if otherwise it will result in a *chupas niddah*.

[3] "When a woman has a discharge — her discharge from her flesh being blood — she shall be in her state of separation for a seven-day period ..." (*Vayikra* 15:19.) "If a woman's blood flows for many days outside of her period of separation, or if she has a flow after her separation, all the days of her discharge-impurity shall be as her days of her separation [menstrual period] ... If she ceases her flow, she must count seven days for herself, and afterwards she can be purified." (*Vayikra* 15:25,28.)

[4] Note that *niddah* bleeding lasted seven days or less. If a "period" lasted more than seven days, it was classified as *zavah*.

In contrast, when discussing the second type of bleeding — called *zavah* blood — the *Torah* requires a woman to wait until all the bleeding has stopped and only then count the required clean day or days before immersing in a *mikveh* and resuming physical contact with her husband. (If she saw one or two days of *zavah* blood, called *zavah katanah*, she was required to wait only one clean day before immersing in a *mikveh*. If she saw more than two days of *zavah* blood, called *zavah gadolah*, she was required to wait seven clean days before immersion.) In general, *zavah* blood included any uterine blood that flowed in the first eleven days after the seven days of the *niddah* separation.[5]

Today, according to Jewish law, all bleeding from the shedding of the lining of the uterus follows the laws of the *zavah gadolah* and not the laws of the *niddah*.[6]

Why don't we distinguish between these two types of bleeding? Seemingly, based on the descriptions given in the *Torah*, it would not be so complicated to determine which is *niddah* and which is *zavah*.

The reason is as follows: According to the *Mishnah*, in addition to the color black, only four specific shades of red (of the many shades of red that blood can be) can make a woman *tamei*, spiritually "impure."[7] But as far back as 1,700 years ago — at the time of the writing of the *Gemara* — the ability to distinguish between these different shades of red was already lost to the Jewish people. It is generally understood that this *mesorah*, tradition, was lost due to the spiritual decline of the Jewish people.[8] Because of this, it became impossible to determine

---

[5]   Part of the Oral Law taught to Moses at Sinai was the laws of the *zavah*. In the first eleven days after a woman's *niddah* separation, uterine blood was classified as *zavah* blood. If the *zavah* blood lasted for three consecutive days, she could only become *niddah* again if she had experienced seven consecutive days free of bleeding (Rashi;Tur *Yoreh Deah* 183). Also, it was only if the *zavah* blood flowed for three days or more (giving her the status of *zavah gadolah*) that seven clean days were required before she immersed in a *mikveh* (*Toras Kohanim* to *Vayikra* 15:25). A *zavah* flow of less than three days (*zavah katanah*) only required one clean day (*Niddah* 73a).

[6]   *Yoreh Deah* 183.

[7]   *Niddah* 19a. See Ch. 3 for a further discussion of this issue.

[8]   *Niddah* 20b; Tur *Yoreh Deah* 188.

with certainty when to begin and end counting the seven days specified in the *Torah* for the *niddah* separation.

To explain, let us take the simplest case — that of a woman with a regular period. She bleeds once every 28 days for five days. However, it is possible that the blood she sees on the first day of her period is not one of the specific shades of red — i.e., it is not *tamei*, spiritually "impure." Until the blood is *tamei*, she does not begin counting the seven days (and, of course, she need not separate from her husband because she is not *niddah*). However, if she accidentally started counting when she was *tahor*, spiritually "clean," she would not have been separated from her husband the required seven days from the start of *tamei* blood flow. She would have immersed in the *mikveh* too soon and still be *niddah* according to *Torah* law.

Before the *mesorah* for distinguishing the different shades of red was completely lost, but at the point of time where the average women could not be certain when she became *niddah*, there was a *takanah*, a rabbinic injunction, made that any woman who had a three-day flow of uterine blood must wait for seven consecutive clean days before immersing in a *mikveh*.[9]

Later, the women themselves adopted the practice of waiting seven clean days under all circumstances.[10] Because this practice was universally accepted by Jewish women (giving it the status of a *takana*),[11] it had (and has today) the force of *halachah*. When a practice becomes universally accepted and thus followed by the Jewish people, it is considered binding in Jewish law because of the principle of *al titosh toras imecha*, do not forsake the teaching of your mother.[12] This means that a practice or custom universally accepted by the Jewish people has a status

---

9   After the *mesorah* was lost, but before the women themselves adopted the additional *takanah* of waiting seven clean days under all circumstances (see text), if a woman bled for less than three days, she only had to wait six clean days (see *Niddah* 66a), since whether she was a *niddah* or a *zavah ketanah*, she would be covered. If she was a *niddah*, the worst case was that the last day of her flow was really her first *niddah* day. If she was not a *niddah* but a *zavah*, then she really needed only one clean day (as per the laws of the *zavah ketanah*).

10   *Niddah* 66a.

11   Ibid.

12   *Mishlei* 11:1.

of a vow that is binding on all their descendents.[13] ("Mother" in this verse is understood by our Sages to mean the Jewish people.[14])

To this day, there is no leniency in *halachah* that allows a woman to wait only the seven days (from when her bleeding began) before going to the *mikveh*. She must wait seven consecutive days free from all bleeding.[15]

The Five Days

Our next discussion concerns why we wait a minimum of five days before we begin to count the Seven Clean Days.

The *Gemara* relates that part of the Oral Law that was given to Moses at Mount Sinai said that the clean days of the *zavah* must be free not only from any discharge of blood but also from any discharge of live semen.[16] Live semen is defined as that which is capable of producing a child.[17] The *Gemara* also says that semen can stay alive up to 72 hours inside a woman's body.[18] It is interesting to note that modern science has recently discovered this fact, which was known to our Sages thousands of years ago.

Now let us take the case of a woman who had relations with her husband during the night and experienced a discharge of *zavah* blood the next day. The flow lasted less than one day. However, on the third day after the relations had taken place, there might still be live semen present in her body. Therefore, she was not able to start counting her clean days within 72 hours of having relations, since it was assumed that she could have an emission of semen in that time of

---

[13] *Pesachim* 50b.

[14] *Brachos* 35b.

[15] *Niddah* 66a.

[16] If any discharge of semen occurred during the Seven Clean Days, it would invalidate the count, but for that day only (*Niddah* 22a; *Yoreh Deah* 196:11). This is in contrast to the *halachah* which says that if a woman sees any blood during the Seven Clean Days, she must start counting again until she has counted seven consecutive clean days (*Niddah* 22a).

[17] *Shabbos* 86a.

[18] Ibid.

which she was unaware. Since it was impractical to calculate these 72 hours from the precise time that relations took place, it became the practice to wait three full days after the bleeding began before starting the count of the Seven Clean Days[19] — meaning that the woman would check herself on the fourth day, and the count would begin on the fifth day.[20]

Later, *Ashkenazi* women adopted the practice to wait one more day,[21] meaning that the check would take place on the fifth day (after which the Seven Clean Days are counted).[22]

Regardless of whether or not a couple had relations in the days right before the wife got her period (or began to bleed for some other reason that would make her *niddah*), the practice among *Ashkenazi* woman became to always wait five days before counting the Seven Clean Days. Since these practices were universally adopted, they are *halachah* today for *Ashkenazi* Jews.[23] However, if a woman is having trouble conceiving because she ovulates before she can go to the *mikveh*, she

---

[19] *Terumas HaDeshen*, 14th century. This was based on the assumption that people do not keep track of the precise time they had relations. Rama cites this as *halachah* (*Yoreh Deah* 196:11). However, there are prominent *Ashkenazi halachic* authorities that rule leniently (i.e., not to be concerned about this custom (or the fifth day) under extenuating circumstance (see *Pischei Teshuvah* 196:15, citing *Shelah* and *Sidrei Taharah*). Depending on their country of origin, *Sefardim* are not necessarily strict about this. See Rav Ovadiah Yosef (*Taharas HaBayis* Vol. 2, pg. 405).

[20] This is why a woman before her wedding is allowed to check herself as soon as her period stops if she bleeds less than five days. (*Taz Yoreh Deah* 196:7). *Shach Yoreh Deah* 196:20 rules this way only under extenuating circumstances, for example, if otherwise it will result in a *chupas niddah*. It is assumed she is not having relations, and therefore, there is no concern about an emission of semen invalidating the Seven Clean Days.

[21] This was a *takanah* reported by *Trumas HaDeshen* 245. *Trumas HaDeshen* mentions it as an existent practice. His wording seems to imply that in his day it was not yet universally accepted. Rama, *Yoreh Deah* 196:11 quotes it but also not as universal practice.

[22] Rama says, as does *Trumas HaDeshen*, that the reason for this practice is to prevent making a mistake in the count in case the woman had begun to bleed at twilight (between sunset and nightfall, when it is a question as to which Jewish day it is).

[23] Rama, *Yoreh Deah* 196:11. *Trumas HaDeshen* 245 reports that this was originally a stringency adopted by *Ashkenazi* Jews.

should consult her *halachic* authority as there are certain leniencies which might permit her to shorten these five days.

Various customs exist among *Sefardi* Jews depending on their country of origin.[24]

---

[24] Rav Ovadiah Yosef (*Taharas HaBayis* Vol. 2. pg. 402). For example, in Baghdad and Salonica, Rav Odadiah relates that the custom was to wait five days, but in Syria, Egypt and Israel (Palestine) it wasn't. Rav Ovadiah rules that Sephardi women do not need to keep a fifth day. Another practice of waiting six or seven days is mentioned by certain *rishonim*, but they themselves (the *rishonim*), object to it (see *Taharas HaBayis* Vol. 2. pg. 402).

CHAPTER 6

♦

Counting the Seven Clean Days

As we saw in the previous chapter, the Seven Clean Days are of great importance in the *halachos* governing Family Purity. Therefore, it is essential to count
them properly.[1] In this chapter, we will discuss *halachos* of the Seven Clean Days
and the days leading into them.

The Hefsek Taharah

Before counting the Seven Clean Days, it is first necessary to be sure that your
period is truly over. To accomplish this, a special check, called the *hefsek taharah*,[2]
is done.[3] Without this special check, it is impossible to begin counting the Seven
Clean Days and immerse in the *mikveh*.[4]

Why is the *hefsek* so important? Once you begin bleeding, you have the "status" of a woman who is bleeding. This is because there exists a concept in *halachah*
called *chazakah*, roughly translated as "status quo."[5] To begin counting the Seven

---

1   Otherwise a woman may immerse in the *mikveh* and mistakenly believe she is no longer
    niddah, when in fact, her status has not changed.
2   *Hefsek* literally means "break;" *taharah* means "spiritual purity."
3   *Yoreh Deah* 196:1.
4   *Yoreh Deah* 196:5.
5   *Niddah* 68b.

Clean Days, you must change this status. Thus, the purpose of the *hefsek taharah* is to change your status, or *chazakah*, by showing both that the bleeding has stopped and that you don't expect it any more.[6]

This check is accomplished by taking a small, soft, white cloth, wrapping it around your index finger and inserting it internally. The cloth should be gently pressed outwards in a circular motion, so that all the inner crevices and accordion folds of the vagina are checked. Thus, if you can see that there is no blood anywhere after making such a thorough check, then you also know that the bleeding has already stopped for a while.

Ready-made packages of *bedikah* cloths can be purchased in most *mikveh* houses, or you can make your own. The cloth should be 7-8 centimeters squared or about three inches squared[7] and be completely white.

If you experience trouble getting a *hefsek taharah* that is free from any *niddah* colors, it could be that the blood you are seeing is coming from a wound or other internal irritation, which is being aggravated by the *bedikah* cloth. Please read carefully the section below, *Difficulties Obtaining a Hefsek Taharah Free From Niddah Colors*.

Color on a Bedikah Cloth

As we discussed in Chapter 3, your *bedikah* cloth does not have to come out white. It only has to come out free from any colors that render a woman *niddah*. (See Ch. 3 for guidelines regarding colors.)

Viewing Colors Accurately

Remember that to see a color on a *bedikah* cloth accurately, it should be put on top of something white and viewed in indirect natural daylight (or, if necessary,

---

[6]   It is because of the concept of *chazakah* that a woman does not have to check herself every day after going to the *mikveh*. Once she has gone to the *mikveh*, she has the status of being *tahor*, spiritually "pure," and remains so until the next time she bleeds. (However, during the day, or days, she is expecting her period, there are certain times when she must check herself. For further discussion, see Ch. 10.)

[7]   *Shiurei Shevet HaLevi* 196:6:1. See also Rabbi Shimon Eider, *Halachos of Niddah* pg. 64.

non-natural light) without glasses. However, non-natural light makes most colors appear darker.

In addition, make sure you pre-check your *bedikah* cloths carefully before using them to be certain that they don't have red or black threads accidentally woven into them.

Asking Questions

After making a *bedikah*, if you do see a questionable color on your cloth, do not hesitate to consult an expert in this area of Jewish law — don't just assume your *bedikah* is not good. Let the cloth dry then save it in a clean envelope until you can have the question resolved. Mark on the envelope which *bedikah* it was, for example, the *hefsek taharah*, etc. Avoid putting the cloth in an air-tight plastic bag or waiting more than 48 hours (if possible) to ask your question, as the colors can change.

Questions about *bedikos* can be answered with the utmost privacy and dignity. If you need help finding a Rav to whom these questions can be asked, ask your Rebbetzin or a knowledgeable, observant woman with whom you are friendly for advice. Asking questions on these matters is a normal part of Jewish life; not asking questions about *bedikah* cloths (or other matters concerning the Laws of Family Purity) can unnecessarily prolong the separation time between you and your husband.

Signs of a Wound

If your period just doesn't seem to end (or you see red blood either during the Seven Clean Days or any other time when you aren't expecting your period), it's wise to consult a doctor, nurse, midwife or a trained practitioner to find out the source of the bleeding.[8] In many communities, *"niddah* nurses" (called *bodkos* in Hebrew) are available. These are *Torah*-observant women nurses who have been

---

[8]   Abnormal bleeding is very often an indication of a wound in the tissue. It can also signal a hormonal imbalance or serious illness, which if caught in the early stages, need not be life threatening.

trained to locate the source of bleeding. If you have a wound that is bleeding, it may be necessary for the *niddah* nurse to make the *hefsek taharah* for you. A small wound — which would not necessarily be felt — on the outside of the cervix or in the wall of vagina (common occurrences) can bleed for many days, even weeks. Wounds are particularly irritated by foreign objects such a *bedikah* cloth or tampon.

As we discussed in Chapter 3, blood that results from a wound is not *niddah* blood. For more information on how to count the Seven Clean Days with a wound that is bleeding so that you can go to the *mikveh* on time, see below.

Preparation for the Hefsek Taharah

Before doing the *hefsek taharah*, clean yourself so that if you do find blood, you know that it is fresh and not old blood. Indeed, this cleansing is considered a *mitzvah*.[9] To this end, many women have adopted the practice of taking a bath or shower and changing into white undergarments before making their *hefsek taharah*.

However, it is adequate to simply wash the relevant areas. Under extenuating circumstance (such as travel), you may make a *hefsek taharah* without washing yourself.[10]

If you work during the day, you may wash yourself at home and make your *hefsek taharah* early in the day before you leave your house (see footnote for the proper procedure if you saw blood that day prior to making your *hefsek*).[11]

Cleaning Internally

Depending on your body, you may need to clean internally before doing the *hefsek taharah* to wash away any residue from old blood. This can be done either by douching or simply using a dampened *bedikah* cloth. Make sure if you do clean

---

9   Rama, *Yoreh Deah* 196:3.
10   Ibid. See also *Badei HaShulchan* ad loc. *Biurim* s.v. *Uminhag*.
11   *Shiurei Shevet HaLevi* 196:10. The *moch* (the special check that is made by inserting a *bedikah* cloth internally just before sunset and removing it after nightfall) is then made at the normal time. If she saw blood that day (prior to the *hefsek*), she should make sure to make a *bedikah* with the *moch* as she inserts it.

internally, that it is done in a gentle manner so as not to irritate or dry out your body's natural lubrication. (It is at this point in a woman's cycle that her natural fluids are thinnest; thus the tissue can be more susceptible to wounds.)

In addition, if you clean internally, you will need to wait some time — preferably 15 minutes — before doing the *hefsek taharah*.[12] If you are pressed for time (for example, it is right before sunset), you may clean internally and then make your *hefsek taharah* immediately afterwards.[13]

On Shabbos or Yom Tov

If your day to make the *hefsek taharah* falls on *Shabbos* or *Yom Tov*, simply clean the relevant areas before making your *hefsek taharah*, taking care not to violate the special prohibitions of the day. For example, you may wash but not with a wash cloth.[14] On *Shabbos*, if you would like to wash with warm water, you will need to use water that was heated before *Shabbos* began (for example, from your *Shabbos* kettle).

You may — and should — make a *hefsek taharah* on *Yom Kippur*, *Tishah B'Av*, and during the Nine Days of mourning preceding *Tishah B'Av*.[15] A woman who is sitting *shivah* may (and should) make a *hefsek taharah*. Since bathing is prohibited on these days, only the necessary areas should be washed; however, warm water may be used.[16] On *Yom Kippur*, you will need to use water heated before *Yom Kippur* began.

When to Make the Hefsek Taharah

The earliest time that the *hefsek* may be done is on the fifth day after your period began, counting as "Day One" the day your period began. (See footnote

---

[12] *Igros Moshe Yoreh Deah* 2:71.
[13] *Shiurei Shevet HaLevi* 196:3:4.
[14] If it is your practice to take a bath before the *hefsek*, you may do so on *Shabbos* or *Yom Tov* but only in cool water (*Shach* 199:12).
[15] *Shach* 199:12; *Shaar HaTziyun* 551:35.
[16] *Shach* 199:12; see also *Shach Yoreh Deah* 381:3 and *Taz* ad loc. 381:2.

below for exceptions to this rule.[17]) The best time to make the *hefsek* is in the late afternoon close to sunset.[18] If the need arises, you may do your *hefsek taharah* earlier.[19] However, since the Jewish day begins at sunset, you must do your *hefsek*, and thus change your "status," before sunset. If your period lasts longer than five days, wait until you see that it is over and make your *hefsek taharah* that day (before sunset).

If the bleeding has completely stopped when you wake up on the day you will be making your *hefsek*, make a thorough *bedikah* first thing in the morning (or when you see that the bleeding has stopped). That way, if the day becomes hectic, and you get distracted and forget to make your *hefsek taharah* before sunset, this *bedikah* can count (after the fact) as your *hefsek taharah*.[20]

If you forget to do your *hefsek* altogether until after sunset, but it is still close to sunset, make a *hefsek*, note the exact time it was made, and then consult your *halachic* authority. Depending on the time and place, it may be acceptable.[21]

If you are still bleeding during the day but want to try to get a clean *hefsek* before sunset, you are allowed to make as many checks as you want. However,

---

[17] With the following exceptions: If you see blood during the Seven Clean Days, you do not need to wait five days before making the *hefsek taharah* (since you have already done that). Also, if a woman finishes all bleeding from her period, for example, by the third or fourth day and has a wound that usually bleeds on the fifth day due to a decrease in her natural lubrication, she may make her *hefsek taharah* as soon as the bleeding has stopped (*Yoreh Deah* 196:11). However, she cannot begin her count of the Seven Clean Days until these five days have passed. A woman who ovulates before she can immerse in the *mikveh* should consult her *halachic* authority regarding these five days.

[18] *Yoreh Deah* 196:1.

[19] *Beis Yosef, Yoreh Deah* 196 mentions from the time of minchah *katanah*. This is two and a half daylight hours before sunset. The normally accepted method of calculating daylight hours is to take the length of the day between sunrise and sunset (in hours and minutes) and divide it by 12. Thus, a daylight hour is longer in the summer and shorter in the winter. In addition, *Shiurei Shevet HaLevi* 196:10 says, "Women who work and cannot bathe prior to making a *hefsek taharah* should wash themselves and make the *hefsek taharah* early in the day at home and in the afternoon should insert the *moch dachuk*. If she had seen blood that day (prior to the *hefsek*), she should make sure to make a *bedikah* with the *moch* as she inserts it."

[20] Based on Rama, *Yoreh Deah* 196:1.

[21] The *halachic* leeway regarding sunset depends on how close your location is to the equator (which effects how quickly the sun sets). It also depends on local *halachic* custom.

doing a lot of thorough checking with a *bedikah* cloth can be irritating and even cause bleeding. (Although this would not qualify as *niddah* blood, you wouldn't be able to tell the difference at this point.)

In general, if you see a small speck of a questionable color on your *bedikah* cloth, make another *hefsek* and see if the color is still present. But if you see a large stain of a questionable color on the cloth, it's usually better not to make many checks over and over again. Rather, show the *bedikah* cloth to a competent *halachic* authority. Also, keep in mind when doing multiple checks, you will need to wait between them, for fifteen minutes if possible. (See above, *Preparation for the Hefsek Taharah.*)

The Moch Dachuk

After completing your *hefsek taharah*, the next step is the *moch dachuk* (an in-serted cloth). The *moch* is a special check that is accomplished by inserting a *bedikah* cloth internally just before sunset and removing it after nightfall (when you can see three stars in the sky). As in the case of the *hefsek taharah*, the special check of the *moch* is done on the fifth day of your period (or on a subsequent day, if your period lasts longer).

What is the purpose of the *moch* and why do we make such a check? As we discussed above, the purpose of the *hefsek taharah* is to change your *chazakah*, or status. The *moch* accomplishes the same thing, but since it is done during the last moments of the day, you know for certain that the (Jewish) day has ended with no more bleeding. The *moch* is the equivalent of making a *bedikah* over the entire period of time when the Jewish day is ending.

Under normal circumstances, every woman should endeavor to insert a *moch*.[22] The *moch* should preferably be kept in until nightfall (roughly the time that *Shabbos* is over). A woman who finds this difficult should consult her *halachic* authority.[23]

---

[22] *Yoreh Deah* 196:1. Even though making a *moch* is the normative practice, it is only required when a woman is making her *hefsek taharah* on the first day that she saw the bleeding (for example, if she saw blood during the Seven Clean Days). If making a *moch* causes a woman irritation or bleeding, she should consult a *halachic* authority.

[23] *Badei HaShulchan* 196:21 rules if this is difficult or uncomfortable, it need not be kept in so

In addition, there are a number of circumstances where doing the *moch* might cause a woman irritation, pain, or even bleeding. For example, a woman who has very sensitive skin, a woman after childbirth or a gynecological procedure, a woman who experiences pain during her *hefsek taharah* or, most commonly, a woman who has a wound (or a suspected wound) in her vagina or cervix. If you find yourself in any of the above (or similar) circumstances, consult your *halachic* authority before doing a *moch*.

On *Shabbos*, you may not go outside in an area without an eruv with a *moch* inserted, since it is considered "carrying" (one of the forbidden acts of *Shabbos*).[24]

If you forgot to make a *moch* (or if it fell out), you may still begin counting the Seven Clean Days.

When the Moch Can Count As the Hefsek Taharah

Although there is no requirement to do so, it is a good idea to turn the *bedikah* cloth internally when inserting the *moch*[25] if there is a questionable color on the *hefsek taharah*. That way, if it turns out that the color on the *hefsek* is indeed a *niddah* color, the *moch* can also count as the *hefsek* if it comes out free from any *niddah* color.[26]

Similarly, if one forgot to do a *hefsek taharah*, but did a *moch* (which was inserted before sunset and turned upon insertion), the *moch* can also count as the *hefsek*.[27]

---

long. *Igros Moshe Yoreh Deah* 2:79 says one need not keep the *moch* in for more than 50 minutes after sunset in America, (in Israel, 35 minutes); however, if it is somewhat difficult, but not very difficult, one need only leave in the *moch* for 15 minutes.

24 See *Igros Moshe Orach Chayim* 3:47; *Shu't Minchas Yitzchak* 4:28:9 and 5:37; and *Shiurei Shevet HaLevi* 196:1:13. Note that there is a difference (as far as whether it is considered "carrying" on *Shabbos*) between a *moch* and a tampon or sanitary napkin, that are used to keep one's body clean. Both of the latter are not considered carrying.

25 *Shiurei Shevet HaLevi* 196:1:13, however, he points out that *Chavos Daas* 191:8 does not seem to hold this way.

26 See *Chavos Daas* 191:8 and *Shiurei Shevet HaLevi* 196:1:13.

27 *Shiurei Shevet HaLevi*, Ibid. Even if the *hefsek taharah* was definitely a *niddah* color, but a *moch*

Difficulties Obtaining a Hefsek Taharah
Free From Niddah Colors

If you experience trouble getting a clean *hefsek taharah* or *moch*, it may be that the blood is coming from an irritation or wound in the cervical or vaginal tissue and not from the uterus.

As we discussed in Chapter 3, tissue comprising these parts of the body can become irritated enough to bleed from a number of causes including simple wounds, infection, erosion, exposure to synthetic hormones (including DES) and scratches from foreign objects like tampons and *bedikah* cloths. Sometimes — but not always — the color of the blood will be slightly different from menstrual blood (for example, a brighter red changing to a pinkish color is often an indication of a wound that is healing). Irritations are capable of bleeding for long periods of time and can produce significant quantities of blood.

If you cannot get a *hefsek taharah* free of any *niddah* colors (or even if you do, you are then unable to get a clean *moch*), an irritation, wound or the like may be the cause. Do not hesitate to see a competent practitioner who is experienced in checking for these kinds of problems. Find a practitioner who comes recommended as a person willing to take the time to do a proper examination to locate the source of the problem. In many communities, observant women, who are usually also nurses and/or midwives have been trained as "*niddah* nurses," *bodkos*, for this purpose. Ask if a *niddah* nurse is available in your area. Otherwise, try a midwife or doctor.

If it can be determined that the bleeding is coming solely from this irritation and not from the uterus, there are ways according to *halachah* to count the Seven Clean Days and go to the *mikveh* on time.[28] If you have a wound that is bleeding, it may be necessary for your practitioner to make the *hefsek taharah* for you. See below the section on *Counting the Seven Clean Days With a Wound That Is Bleeding* for a

---

was inserted and turned before sunset and came out free of any *niddah* color, the *moch* can count as the *hefsek*.

[28] See Ch. 3 for a detailed discussion of what constitutes *niddah* blood.

discussion of these *halachos*. Below you will find a discussion on ways to cause less irritation while making *bedikos*.

Making Bedikos Easier

If you experience pain, irritation or bleeding from making *bedikos*, try the following suggestions:

- Slightly dampen the *bedikah* cloth before using it.[29] (This may not be done on *Shabbos* or *Yom Tov*.)

- Apply a clear, water-soluble lubricant (such as K-Y Jelly) to the vaginal opening.[30] This type of lubricant can also be used on *Shabbos* and *Yom Tov*.[31]

- Make sure you are not making contact with the cervix while making your *bedikos*.[32] If you have cervical erosion (a common condition of which you may be unaware) or have been exposed to synthetic hormones such as DES, insert-

---

[29] *Shu't Maharsham* 1:146 cites the following reasons for allowing the *bedikah* cloth to be dampened: (1) Rama states that a woman should wash herself (*Yoreh Deah* 196:3) before she makes a *hefsek taharah*. He does not state that she must dry herself afterwards, which means that her vaginal area is still wet when she makes her *bedikos*, and we are not concerned that water will either dissolve the blood or hide (mask) it. (2) If a woman is uncomfortable, she will not make her *bedikah* properly. Better to put water on the cloth and make a more thorough *bedikah*. (3) If we are concerned that the water will mask or dissolve the blood, then she should be required (according to *halachah*) to wipe herself well before passing urine before making a *bedikah*. Since nowhere in *halachah* is such a requirement mentioned, we must conclude that it is not required. Water should be the same. (Note that *Yoreh Deah* 188:4 says that if a piece of something of undetermined origin left a woman's body, one can tell if it is blood by soaking it for 24 hours in lukewarm water. If it dissolves, then we assume that it is blood. This case is not the same as dampening a *bedikah* cloth.)

[30] A water-soluble lubricant has the same physical effect as using water on a *bedikah* cloth.

[31] Since this does not violate the prohibition of *memachek*, smoothing a surface on *Shabbos*. See *Nimla Tal, Meleches Memachek* 77; *Shiurei Shevet HaLevi* 196:6:8 permits applying vaseline an hour or two before the *bedikah*, (however, this may not be done on *Shabbos* or *Yom Tov*). *Badei HaShulchan* 196:90 prohibits applying ointment into the vaginal area.

[32] *Shiurei Shevet HaLevi* 196:6:8.

ing the *bedikah* cloth deep into the vagina so that it makes contact with the cervix can cause the tissue to bleed.

♦ Wash and dry your *bedikah* cloths before using them. Some women with extremely sensitive skin find the bleach used on commercial *bedikah* cloths very irritating. (Put them in a netted bag and then in the washing machine.)

♦ Take extra care with *bedikos* after childbirth. If you have had stitches, your *bedikos* must be made in a very gentle manner. Otherwise, you may inadvertently open up the incision. Use lubrication (see above) and consult a *halachic* authority as to how many *bedikos* you should be doing during the Seven Clean Days, and if you should do a *moch*.[33]

In general, any kind of wound or irritation of the cervical or vaginal tissue can bleed if irritated by a *bedikah* cloth. During the week after a woman's period, the natural secretions of the vagina are thinner, making it easier to irritate the tissue.

For someone who has had no trouble with the *hefsek taharah*, but then experiences bleeding during the Seven Clean Days, a wound should be suspected. An examination should be done by a specially trained practitioner (*niddah* nurse, midwife or doctor) so that the cause of the bleeding can be determined.

The Seven Clean Days: An Overview

Before going to the *mikveh*, a woman must experience consecutive days without bleeding. These days, referred to as the *Shivah Nekiyim* or "Seven Clean Days," begin on the first (Jewish) day after the *hefsek taharah* was made. An easy way to remember when the seven days are finished is that the *mikveh* night always falls out on the same day of the week that the *hefsek taharah* was made. For example, if the *hefsek* was made on a Tuesday (before sunset), the *mikveh* night will be on the following Tuesday (after nightfall). Since the Jewish day begins at sunset, the

---

[33]   *Shu't Noda BiYehudah* 2:129.

hefsek taharah must be made *before* sunset so that seven full days will be experienced.[34]

During these seven days, internal checks with a *bedikah* cloth are made two times a day, once in the morning and once in the late afternoon (before sunset).[35] These checks are done in the same way as the *hefsek taharah* — by taking a *bedikah* cloth, wrapping it around the index finger and inserting it gently in a circular motion (while pressing outwards).

If you find that doing two checks per day is painful, causes irritation or even bleeding, consult a *halachic* authority (see also above *Making Bedikos Easier*).[36]

Missing a Bedikah During the Seven Clean Days

Although we endeavor not to forget or miss making any of the *bedikos*, in general, missing a *bedikah* during the Seven Clean Days does not invalidate the count. However, the following are three crucial *bedikos*:

- ♦ the *hefsek taharah*,
- ♦ at least one *bedikah* on the first of the Seven Clean Days, and
- ♦ at least one *bedikah* on the seventh day.[37]

---

[34] If shortly after sunset, a woman remembers that she forgot to make her *hefsek taharah*, she should make a *hefsek* immediately, note the exact time it was made and then consult her *halachic* authority.

[35] *Yoreh Deah* 196:4.

[36] In these cases, there are *halachic* leniencies that permit making the minimum amount of *bedikos* necessary, that is, the *hefsek taharah*, one *bedikah* on the first day, one *bedikah* on the seventh day. *Shu't Noda BiYehudah* 2:129 (who also notes that preferably the outside surface should be wiped on the days a *bedikah* is not being made, in place of the *bedikah* that is being omitted).

[37] If a woman forgot to make her morning *bedikah*, but made the evening *bedikah* after sunset but before the time of tzeis (nightfall), she may still go to the *mikveh* on time (*Shiurei Shevet HaLevi* 196:4:9). However, she should consult her *halachic* authority as to the proper time of tzeis. If no *bedikos* were made on the seventh day, a *halachic* authority needs to be consulted (with the exception discussed in Ch. 6, *Counting the Seven Clean Days With a Wound That Is Bleeding*).

Missing any one of these checks *may* push off your *mikveh* date. Always ask a question to a *halachic* authority if you miss one of the above *bedikos*.

Wearing White

Many centuries ago, women apparently wore robes with loose-fitting undergarments. During the Seven Clean Days they changed to white undergarments and slept on white sheets, assuring that if there was any bleeding, it would be seen.[38]

Today, since our undergarments fit quite snugly, *halachah* only requires a woman to wear white underwear during the Seven Clean Days,[39] since any bleeding will be immediately noticeable on it.[40] It is also the practice — *minhag Israel* — to sleep on white sheets.[41] Some *halachic* authorities also say that it is preferable to sleep in a white nightgown.

---

[38] The *Gemara* (*Kesubos* 72a) implies that women wore certain outer garments when they were *niddos*. The white garments they wore were loose-fitting undergarments. (See also *Shiurei Shevet HaLevi* 196:3:3; *Badei HaShulchan* 196:46.) The white sheets were because they slept at night au natural (*Shiurei Shevet HaLevi* 196:3:3). It was not (and is not) considered immodest that others know that a woman is *niddah*. See *Igros Moshe Yoreh Deah* 2:77 who states that all the neighbors knew when a woman was *niddah*. This is indeed implied by the *Gemara* (*Kesubos* 72a). What was considered immodest was to advertise when she was going to the *mikveh*, even though others would figure it out since she would not be wearing her *niddah* garments after she immersed. There is evidence in the *Gemara* that (mature) daughters were aware when their mothers went to the *mikveh*.

[39] *Shiurei Shevet HaLevi* 196:3:3.

[40] *Darchei Chachmah* 117:16 rules that if a woman wore colored underwear during the Seven Clean Days, the count is still good. *Chochmas Adam* 117:8 rules that if she had no whites to wear, the Seven Clean Days are fine. However, if a woman did not wear white during the Seven Clean Days when she could have (for example, she forgot or she did not make them available) that she should be penalized. *Badei HaShulchan* explains *Chochmas Adam* to mean that those days do not count. *Darchei Chachmah* disagrees, explaining that *Chochmas Adam* means that if she finds a stain on her colored undergarment, we must penalize her and say that the stain is not good, even though we would usually permit a stain on colored undergarment. *Toras HaShelamim* 196:8 implies that if she wore colored underwear it is not good, since one cannot tell if she has any stains. A woman should ask a question to her *halachic* authority if she wore colored undergarments during the Seven Clean Days and found a stain on them.

[41] *Shiurei Shevet HaLevi* 196:3:3. If sleeping in underwear irritates your skin, causes you to get a

White undergarments should be totally white with no pattern (except white on white).[42] The time to switch to white undergarments is after the *hefsek taharah* is made and before the *moch* is inserted.[43]

Bathing, Showering and Swimming During the Seven Clean Days

During the Seven Clean Days, a woman is allowed to shower and bathe as normal.[44] However, she is not allowed to clean herself internally or douche to prevent a stain from being found.[45] (If cleaning internally is necessary for medical reasons, the *bedikah* should be done first.[46])

Swimming is fine during the Seven Clean Days.[47] (The lining of your bathing suit does not have to be white.)

Counting the Seven Clean Days

Counting the Seven Clean Days is based on the verse in *Torah* which says, "She shall count seven days for herself,"[48] which the *Gemara* interprets as a requirement for a woman to have an "awareness" that she is in the Seven Clean Days.[49] Some authorities rule that any day that she does not have this awareness does not count as part of the seven days, while others disagree.[50]

---

yeast infection, or is simply uncomfortable, you are not required to sleep in underwear during the Seven Clean Days. However, in this case, you must use white sheets.

[42] Since in our time we rely solely on white underwear and don't wear white robes, etc., the underwear should be totally white.

[43] *Yoreh Deah* 196:3.

[44] *Igros Moshe Yoreh Deah* 1:94 and end of *Yoreh Deah* 2:71.

[45] *Igros Moshe Yoreh Deah* end of 2:71.

[46] *Shu't Maharsham* 2:40; *Igros Moshe Yoreh Deah* 1:94.

[47] *Igros Moshe Yoreh Deah* 1:94 and end of *Yoreh Deah* 2:71.

[48] *Vayikra* 15:28.

[49] *Kesubos* 72a; *Niddah* 68b.

[50] *Me'il Tzedakah* (as quoted by *Sidrei Taharah* 196:18) contends that what makes these days into a unit of "Seven Clean Days" is the fact that she knows that she wants to become *tahorah* and

Although some women have a custom to actually enumerate the seven days, it is not required according to *halachah*. Moreover, many *halachic* authorities explicitly rule that the days are not individually counted.[51]

What does this awareness mean in practical terms? Simply that you *think* you are in the Seven Days, that is, you consider yourself in the Seven Days. Let's take an example to illustrate what this "awareness" means:

After doing one of her *bedikos*, a woman finds what she thinks is blood on the cloth. She puts the cloth aside and decides she is no longer in the Seven Days. Later in the day, just before sunset, she does another *hefsek taharah* so that she can begin counting the days anew. Meanwhile, the next day, she changes her mind about the cloth and decides to ask a question to her *halachic* authority about it. The answer comes back that the color was not *niddah*. But, since she didn't *think*

---

therefore pays attention for all seven days. *Lechem VeSimlah* (*Simlah* 196:7 and 13) disagrees, as do others. The *halachic* question on this position is that a *shotah*, a woman who is *halachically* not responsible for her actions can become *tahorah*. For example, a man marries a woman and she then goes crazy or suffers severe brain damage. The husband is still permitted to live with his wife (*Yoreh Deah* 196:8). How does she become *tahorah* from her *niddah* status? Other women check her *bedikos*. But such a woman is unaware of her body functions or status, so how can you ever say that she has seven clean days? This question is asked by the disputants of the *Me'il Tzedakah* who rule that if a woman decided during her Seven Clean Days that she was unclean, and then realized that she made a mistake, that she has not undone her count. *Shu't Maharsham* 3:114 follows a compromise position: If she went an entire day thinking she was *temei'ah*, it is not good, but a partial day can still be counted. *Shiurei Shevet HaLevi* 196:4 has a lengthy explanation of the subject and rules like Maharsham.

51 *Shelah* holds that it is a *mitzvah* to count each day. He is quoted by *Sidrei Taharah* 196:18 as saying, "I instructed my wife that every evening before sunset she should recite, "Today is the first day of my counting my clean days," "Today is the second day of my counting my clean days," etc." See also *Shelah HaKodesh* (pg. 101a in old edition, quoted by *Pischei Teshuvah* 196:4). This opinion is mentioned by several prominent later authorities, such as *Sidrei Taharah*, *Chochmas Adam* 117:14 who rules like *Shelah*. However, *Shu't Noda BiYehudah* II *Yoreh Deah* 123, *Sidrei Taharah*, and *Pischei Teshuvah* 196:4 point out that no other authorities record a *mitzvah* of "counting" the Seven Clean Days, and that the accepted practice is not to "count" the seven days the way *Shelah* feels one should. *Pischei Teshuvah* cites early authorities (pre-*Shelah*), specifically Maharam Rottenberg and Radbaz, who explicitly rule that one does not count the days the way *Shelah* rules. Among the later *halachic* authorities, *Taharas Yisroel* and *Badei HaShulchan*, for example, do not conclude like *Shelah*. Thus, the majority of other *halachic* authorities do not follow *Shelah*.

she was in the Seven Clean Days, she may now have a *halachic* problem including this particular day[52] in her count and should consult her *halachic* authority. In this case, the woman should have continued her count while she asked her *halachic* authority about the color on the cloth, all the while assuming that it was possible that the color was fine.[53]

If the Mikveh Night is Delayed After the Seven Clean Days

If, for some reason, a woman must delay going to the *mikveh* after she has completed the Seven Clean Days, she is not required to continue wearing white undergarments or making *bedikos*.[54]

Counting the Seven Clean Days With a Wound That Is Bleeding

If you have a wound or irritation that is bleeding, it is still possible to go to the *mikveh* on time. Review the guidelines below and consult your *halachic* authority.

If it can be determined that the blood is coming solely from the wound, you may count Seven Clean Days and go to the *mikveh* on time, if you (or your *niddah* nurse or other practitioner) are able to make a clean *hefsek taharah*.[55] The practitioner has the advantage, in this case, of being able to avoid touching the wound while making the *hefsek*, since the *hefsek* must be made with a cloth.[56]

---

52 Meaning that she would not be required to begin counting from day one again but would only have to wait an extra day (*Pischei Teshuvah* 196:3, quoting *Me'il Tzedakah*). This is in contrast to a woman who finds (uterine) blood during the Seven Clean Days and is required to begin her count anew (*Yoreh Deah* 196:10).

53 *Shiurei Shevet HaLevi* 196:4.

54 As inferred from *Yoreh Deah* 192:2, with the exception of a *kallah* before her wedding. (For more details, see Ch. 11.)

55 *Pischei Teshuvah* 187:32.

56 *Yoreh Deah* 196:6; *Sidrei Taharah* ad loc. 196:22.

If the wound or irritation is close to the opening of the cervix, your practitioner may not be able to determine that the bleeding is coming solely from the irritation and not from the uterus. In this case, you can still go to the *mikveh* on time as long as you can fulfill all of the following conditions:[57]

1. You have confirmation that there exists an irritation that is bleeding;

2. You (or your practitioner) have been able to obtain a clean *hefsek taharah*; and

3. You (or your practitioner) can obtain at least one clean *bedikah* during the Seven Clean Days.

In such situations a *halachic* authority should be consulted.

Finding Niddah Blood During the Seven Clean Days

If you find blood that is coming from the uterus (and not from a wound) during the Seven Clean Days, your count is invalidated. However, you do not have to wait the preliminary five days before counting the Seven Clean Days anew (since you have already waited those five days). As soon the bleeding stops, you can make a new *hefsek taharah* and *moch*, and begin your new count. As we discussed above, if you are making your new *hefsek* on the first day that you began to bleed, you are required to make a *moch*.[58] If making a *moch* causes you irritation or bleeding, consult your *halachic* authority.

---

57   *Pischei Teshuvah* 187:32.
58   *Yoreh Deah* 196:1.

♦

CHAPTER 7

Preparing for the Mikveh

After the end of the Seven Clean Days, there are two more crucial steps necessary before a husband and wife can resume their physical relationship — the wife prepares herself and then immerses in a *mikveh*, a "ritual bath." This immersion is what changes her spiritual status from *tamei*, spiritually "impure," to *tahor*, spiritualy "pure."

Without these steps, the wife remains *niddah*, no matter how many days she has been apart from her husband, how many times she has checked herself, or how many clean days she counted. These steps are essential!

Before explaining the preparation necessary for going to the *mikveh*, we shall examine the principles behind immersion, *tevilah*. Knowledge of these principles will help you tremendously in understanding the laws of *mikveh* preparation and in solving problems, should they arise. Additionally, knowledge of these principles can make going to the *mikveh* a pleasurable, spiritually uplifting experience as opposed to a stressful, nerve-wracking one.

To help you prepare for your immersion on a practical level, you will find a head-to-toe checklist in this chapter.

Principles of Immersion

Tevilah means that you are submerged inside something. Even though the medium of a *mikveh* is water, *tevilah* doesn't have anything to do with washing one-self physically. This is perhaps the biggest proof that a woman who is *niddah* is not considered physically unclean. If that were the case, the *mikveh* would be used as a bath. But *halachah* tells us just the opposite — for a woman to be able to immerse properly in the *mikveh*, she must *first* be physically clean.[1]

Tevilah also means you must be totally enveloped by the *mikveh* water.[2] If, for example, a strand of your hair floats on top of the water, you have not immersed. Similarly, if something separates your body from the waters of the *mikveh*, you also have not immersed.[3]

This type of separation is called a *chatzitzah*, or "intervention." *Chatzitzah* is a term used to refer to any intervening substance that separates the body from the waters of the *mikveh*. Because of the seriousness of the laws of having marital relations while *niddah*, it is essential to be familiar with the principles of *chatzitzah*, so that you know what actually constitutes an intervening substance.

The Three Levels of Chatzitzah

In *halachah*, there are three levels of *chatzitzah*:

1. *Chatzitzah* that needs to be removed according to *Torah* law;

2. *Chatzitzah* that needs to be removed according to Rabbinic law;

3. Items that are required to be removed, but do not constitute a *chatzitzah* if you forgot or were unable to remove them.

Immersing with a *chatzitzah* that falls under the first two categories invalidates the *tevilah* and necessitates immersing again.

Let us examine each category in more detail:

1. A *chatzitzah*, as defined by *Torah* law, includes any object that covers the *majority* of your hair or the *majority* of your body, *and* there are times when you

---

[1]   Niddah 66b.
[2]   Niddah 67a.
[3]   Eruvin 4b.

wouldn't want it there.[4] For example, according to *Torah* law, your *tevilah* would not be valid if you wore a bathing cap while immersing in the *mikveh*.

2. Our Sages made a fence around this law, extending *chatzitzah* to include (a) anything that covers the *majority* of your hair or the majority of your body *even if* you would never want it removed, or (b) anything that covers a *minority* of your hair or body, but is something either most people — or just you personally — do not want there all the time.[5]

Here are a few examples of this type of *chatzitzah*: Immersing in the *mikveh* with a clip in your hair; immersing with dirt under your fingernails. What about peeling skin from a sunburn, for example? Peeling skin is not a *chatzitzah*, since most women do not find it bothersome enough to want to remove it. However, for a particular woman whom it bothers, it becomes a *chatzitzah*.

3. The last category is an item that covers a minority of the hair or body but is not difficult or painful to remove, and you don't mind it being there. In this case, you are required to remove it so as not to distinguish between different types of intervening substances.[6] However, in contrast to the above two categories of *chatzitzah*, if you discover something on your body from this category after you have immersed, your immersion is valid and you need not immerse again.[7]

If an item in this category is painful to remove or cannot be removed, you may immerse with it.

Principles of Preparing for Tevilah: The Laws of Chafifah[8]

Upon the Jewish people's return to Israel from the Babylonian exile,[9] Ezra the

---

[4]   *Eruvin* 4b.
[5]   *Yoreh Deah* 198:1; *Shach* and *Taz* ad loc.
[6]   Rama, *Yoreh Deah* 198:1.
[7]   Ibid.
[8]   See *Yoreh Deah* 198 for a discussion of the laws regarding preparation for *tevilah*.
[9]   This occurred in the year 350 BCE, approximately 70 years after the destruction by the Babylonians of the First Temple built by King Solomon.

Scholar[10] enacted a system of preparation for the *mikveh* known as the laws of *chafifah*, or "cleansing."[11]

There are three different opinions among our early *halachic* authorities as to what this cleansing actually entails:

1. The hair should be washed in warm water and combed;[12]

2. Folds of the skin and other such susceptible areas should be washed with warm water (for example, under the arms, etc.);[13]

3. The entire body should be washed (in practical terms, by soaking in a warm bath).[14]

Practical *halachah* dictates that when we prepare for the *mikveh*, we fulfill all of the above requirements. If medical or other extenuating circumstances prevent taking a hot bath, a hot shower can be substituted.[15]

The Time for Preparation

There is a difference of opinion among our early *halachic* authorities as to when is the proper time to prepare for the *mikveh*. One opinion contends that the *chafifah* should be done as close to one's immersion as possible. Another states that if these preparations are done right before *tevilah*, they may be done too hastily, therefore, the lengthy cleansing should be done during the day.[16]

Since we are left with two opposing opinions, whenever possible, we fulfill

---

[10]   Ezra the Scholar was a leader of the Jewish people and one of the heads of the *Anshei Kenesses HaGedolah*, Men of the Great Assembly. He lived at the end of the Era of the Prophets and before the period of the *Tannaim* (at the time of the building of the second *Beis HaMikdash*).

[11]   *Bava Kama* 82a. The *Gemara* and Rashi state that these laws were enacted as an extension to the *Torah* requirement of *tevilah*.

[12]   Rashi, Rabbeinu Tam etc. ad loc. only say combed. *Yoreh Deah* 199:1 mentions washing hair.

[13]   *Niddah* 66b and Rashi ad loc.

[14]   Gra to *Yoreh Deah* 199:4.

[15]   *Yoreh Deah* 199:1 Technically speaking, none of the early sources require a "bath," per se. They simply state that a woman must wash herself. To this end, a shower suffices. This is also not mentioned since earlier generations did not have the facilities to take a shower.

[16]   See the discussion in *Niddah* 68a of Rashi and *Tosafos* (where *Tosafos* quotes Rav Achai Gaon as the disputant of Rashi).

both opinions. Practically speaking, this is accomplished by starting the bathing and other preparations during the day and finishing right before immersion (or at least rinsing a second time and re-combing the hair right before immersion).[17]

If it is not possible to begin your preparations in the daytime — for example, if you work and get home after dark in the wintertime — you may do your entire *chafifah* after nightfall as long as you do not rush through your preparations.[18] To insure that you don't hurry, some *halachic* authorities recommend setting aside the amount of time that it normally takes you to do your *chafifah* and spend that same amount of time if you have to prepare entirely at night.[19] Others say that if these preparations have to be done entirely at night, a full hour must be spent on them.[20] Preparations that don't fall under the category of *chafifah* may be done earlier and then rechecked before *tevilah* (for example, cutting the nails).

Tevilah on Shabbos or Yom Tov

Although it is sometimes difficult to prepare for the *mikveh* on a Friday afternoon or the afternoon before a *Yom Tov* (holiday from the *Torah*), it is a *mitzvah* to go to the *mikveh* on time — the first night after the Seven Clean Days finish, as long as your husband is in town.[21]

In addition, postponing going to the *mikveh* sends a very powerful negative message to your husband. Each woman and her husband should arrange their lives in whatever way necessary, so that the wife is able to go to the *mikveh* on time.

Even if the *mikveh* night falls on the second night of a two-day *Yom Tov* or on a *Shabbos* that follows a two-day *Yom Tov*, a woman should not forgo going to the *mikveh* by making the mistake of thinking that there is no way she can stay clean.

---

[17] To fulfill both of these opinions — preparing during the day as well as right before immersion — make sure both of your preparations fall under the *halachic* definition of *chafifah*.

[18] Rama, *Yoreh Deah* 199:3.

[19] Responsa Maharshal 6 cited by *Shach* 199:6.

[20] *Shiurei Shevet HaLevi*, pg. 365.

[21] *Yoreh Deah* 197:2. See Ch. 6 as to when to immerse in the *mikveh* if your husband is out of town.

If your *mikveh* night falls on one of these special nights, review the section above regarding *chatzitzah*. You will find it is entirely possible to meet these requirements even in the middle of a two- or three-day *Yom Tov*. Being familiar with these laws means you can go to the *mikveh* happy and relaxed even on one of these days.

If your *mikveh* night falls on one of these special nights, finish all your preparations before candle lighting (or, if necessary, before sunset). Tie back, clip or pin up your hair so it doesn't become tangled. In general, try to be careful to keep clean and especially avoid sticky substances on your hands. If, after sunset you find that some part of your body needs to be re-washed, you may do so in a way that doesn't break any of the prohibitions of *Shabbos* or *Yom Tov*. When it is time for *tevilah*, go to the *mikveh*.

If you need to drive to the *mikveh* before *Shabbos* or *Yom Tov* (to avoid walking both ways), light candles before you leave. Before lighting, make a declaration that you will not be taking on *Shabbos* with your candle lighting. Leave adequate time to arrive at the *mikveh* before sundown. When you arrive, touch up anything that needs cleaning and take on *Shabbos* before sundown. (If your husband is coming with you so he can accompany you on the walk home, designate a place to meet him afterwards so that he will not see the other women who are using the *mikveh* on the same night.)

In some communities, it is necessary to let the *mikveh* attendant know ahead of time that you will need to immerse on *Shabbos* or *Yom Tov*. This usually can be done simply by calling the *mikveh* or the *mikveh* attendant in advance. (This may also be the procedure for using the *mikveh* in a small community on any night.)

If your *mikveh* night falls on the second (or third) night of a *Yom Tov*, do all your preparations before the *Yom Tov* or *Shabbos* begins and go to the *mikveh* on time. If you find something that needs cleaning, you may do so in a way that doesn't violate any of the special prohibitions of the day. For example, teeth can be cleaned with a dry toothbrush. Dental floss (either pre-cut or used without cutting) can be used if your gums don't normally bleed when you floss. For gums that bleed easily, dental tape may not make them bleed. If your gums bleed even with dental tape, a toothpick may be used.

If you have a question about something that you think might prevent you from immersing on a *Yom Tov* or *Shabbos* night, always ask a competent *halachic* authority; don't just assume that you can't immerse.

Tevilah on the Night
After Shabbos or Yom Tov

If your *mikveh* night falls on a Saturday night or the night after a *Yom Tov*, it is best to do all your preparations before *Shabbos* or *Yom Tov*, if at all possible. When *Shabbos* or *Yom Tov* ends, bathe or shower, comb out your hair and recheck yourself.[22]

If it is not possible to prepare before *Shabbos* or *Yom Tov*, you may make all your preparations afterwards. However, as we discussed above, to make sure you don't hurry through your preparations, designate an amount of time to spend preparing by estimating how much time it usually takes you. Be sure to clean between your teeth extra carefully if you ate meat or chicken on *Shabbos* or *Yom Tov*.

Tevilah on the Night
After a Two- or Three-Day Yom Tov

If your night to go to the *mikveh* falls after a two- or three-day *Yom Tov*, try to make as many of your preparations beforehand as you can, then go over them after the *Yom Tov* ends.[23] If this is not possible, you may prepare entirely afterwards. As we discussed in the above section, to make sure you don't hurry through your preparations, designate an amount of time to spend preparing by estimating how much time it usually takes you. Clean especially well between your teeth if you ate meat or chicken during the *Yom Tov*.

---

[22]   Rama, *Yoreh Deah* 199:4.
[23]   *Shach* 199:6.

When Your Mikveh
Night Falls on Yom Kippur or Tishah B'Av

If your night to immerse in the *mikveh* falls on the night of *Yom Kippur* or *Tishah B'Av*, it is postponed until the following night, since bathing and marital relations are prohibited on these days.

To prepare for immersion on *motzaei Yom Kippur* or *motzaei Tishah B'Av*, follow the procedure above for going to the *mikveh* the evening after *Shabbos*: If at all possible, make all your preparations beforehand (including using warm water even on erev *Tishah B'Av*); after the conclusion of *Yom Kippur* or *Tishah B'Av*, take a shower (and bath, if necessary), comb out your hair and recheck yourself. If it is not possible to prepare beforehand, you may make all your preparations afterward, taking care not to hurry through them, following the procedure that we discussed above.[24]

Tevilah During the First Eight Days
of the Month of Av

If your *mikveh* night falls during the first eight days of the month Av, all preparations are made as usual, including bathing in warm water.

While Sitting Shivah

If a woman's night to go to the *mikveh* falls during a time when she is sitting *shivah*, her immersion is postponed until after the *shivah* is finished. In this case, she also waits to begin her preparations until the *shivah* is finished since both bathing and marital relations are prohibited during this time.[25]

If the husband is sitting *shivah* and his wife's scheduled time to go to the *mikveh* falls during that week, there is a disagreement among *halachic* authorities as to whether or not his wife should go to *mikveh* at the correct time or wait until the *shivah* is over.[26] In this case, the couple should ask their *halachic* authority.

---

[24] *Magen Avraham* 554:10 and *Mishnah Berurah* 554:18.
[25] *Yoreh Deah* 381:5 and *Rama* ad loc.
[26] *Badei HaShulchan* 197:16 quotes this dispute. Those who feel the wife should wait until her

Preparation Checklist

The following is a step-by-step checklist presented in a practical order to help you prepare for the *mikveh*.

Whether you prepare for your *tevilah* at the *mikveh* or at home is a personal decision, which usually depends on many factors and may change from month to month: The atmosphere at home, facilities at your local *mikveh*, time of day you have available to prepare, etc.[27] If you do prepare entirely at home, take a final shower at the *mikveh* and re-comb your hair before immersing, unless it is *Shabbos* or *Yom Tov*.

Seventh Day Bedikah

Make your final *bedikah* for the seventh day before sunset.[28]

Nails

Many women begin their preparations for the *mikveh* by first removing all nail polish, then cutting and shaping their fingernails.[29] This is easier to do when the

---

husband's period of mourning is over are concerned that they may have relations even though he is not permitted (see *Shu't Maharam Shick* 365). Moreover, when one member of a couple is sitting *shivah*, the accepted practice is to refrain from all affectionate contact, although keeping the harchokos is not required (*Yoreh Deah* 383:1 and Rama 383:1). *Pischei Teshuvah* 197:8 rules that a wife may immerse during her husband's period of mourning.

[27] *Badei HaShulchan* 199:42 appears to follow the approach that a woman should make her preparations in the way that is most conducive for her to be able to focus on properly preparing for the *mikveh*. In contrast, there are *halachic* authorities who feel that a woman should deliberately prepare for *tevilah* at the *mikveh* because of the opinion that her *chafifah* should be done immediately before immersion (see *Shiurei Shevet HaLevi* 199:3:5 on *Taz* 5).

[28] If this *bedikah* is forgotten, you can still go to the *mikveh* as long as you made your morning *bedikah*. If you forgot your morning *bedikah*, but made the evening *bedikah* after sunset but before three stars, you may still go to the *mikveh* on time (*Shiurei Shevet HaLevi* 196:4:9). If no *bedikos* were made on the seventh day, a *halachic* authority needs to be consulted (with the exception discussed in Ch. 6, *Counting the Seven Clean Days With a Wound That Is Bleeding*).

[29] Rama, *Yoreh Deah* 198:20 states that since the custom is to trim nails before immersing, that nails are a *chatzitzah*, and that if a woman neglected to trim even one nail she must return to the *mikveh* and immerse again. This is the accepted practice. In addition, since any crack in nail polish is a *chatzitzah*, all nail polish needs to be removed.

fingernails are not soft from soaking in a bath. Toenails are easier to cut once you have soaked for a while and they are a bit soft.[30]

Any dirt under your nails is a *chatzitzah* and must be removed. Because dirt can be difficult to remove from under long nails, the nails are cut short before immersing in the *mikveh*.[31] In addition, since it became a custom to cut the nails before immersion, long nails may be considered *chatzitzah*. If a woman forgot to trim even one nail, she would need to return to the *mikveh* and immerse again.[32] Nails that were cut within three days of immersion do not need to be cut again if they still short enough.[33]

Hanging skin around the nails should be cut before immersion. However, if it is found afterwards, it does not invalidate the immersion.[34] Similarly, if your *tevilah* falls on a Friday or *Yom Tov* night, and after sunset you find skin that is hanging around a nail, you may still immerse.[35]

However, if your *tevilah* falls on *Shabbos* or a *Yom Tov* and you discover a torn nail after sunset, you must ask a non-Jew to remove the broken part of the nail, preferably by pulling it off by hand (rather than by clipping it with nail clippers or scissors).[36] If you discover on *Shabbos* or *Yom Tov*, that you have forgotten to cut a nail, some authorities rule that the procedure is the same as the above with a torn nail while others disagree, contending it is better to immerse with the long nail as long as it is clean.[37]

---

[30]   Although the *Kabbalistic* practice of not cutting the fingernails and toenails the same day is quoted by some *halachic* sources (see *Magen Avraham* 260:1; *Mishnah Berurah* ad loc. 260:6), the practice is that women cut their toenails and fingernails as needed when preparing for the *mikveh*.

[31]   *Yoreh Deah* 198:18 says that dirt under the nail not "opposite the skin" is a *chatzitzah*. However, since it is unclear what is considered "opposite the skin," the custom developed to cut the nails before immersion. Although there is no mention of how short, a good rule is to keep your nails (at least) shorter than the end of your fingertips and short enough that they are strong and won't crack.

[32]   Rama, *Yoreh Deah* 198:20.

[33]   *Chut Shani* 198:29 (5).

[34]   *Chochmas Adam* 119:16.

[35]   Ibid.

[36]   *Nekudos HaKesef* to 198:20; *Magen Avraham* 340:1 *Bi'ur Halachah* 340:1 s.v vichayov.

[37]   *Taz* 198:21 quotes authorities who rule that one should have a non-Jew remove the nail. He

If you have false nails, you must consult a *halachic* authority in advance of your *tevilah*.

Bathing

Before beginning your *chafifah* (cleansing), take off any bandages or anything adhesive you may have on your body, as well as all of your jewelry and make-up; then soak in a hot or warm bath. While you are soaking, you can use the time to:

- ✦ Clean between your toes
- ✦ Clean between the folds of your skin
- ✦ Clean your navel
- ✦ Clean your ears, nose, eyes (see details below)
- ✦ Cut your toenails
- ✦ Clean internally[38]
- ✦ Shampoo your hair

If there is a medical reason (or some other extenuating circumstance) why you cannot take a bath, you can take a hot or warm shower instead.

Ears

Clean your ears inside and out. If you have pierced ears, clean also inside the earring holes (by using a clean earring post or wire from front to back and from back to front).

Face and Eyes

Wash your face thoroughly and remove all traces of make-up. The day you

---

disagrees strongly, contending that under these circumstances she may not ask a non-Jew to remove the nail, but instead she should immerse herself with the long nail.

[38] This may be done by simply using water and your finger. Even though water doesn't normally reach this area, it must also be free of *chatzitzah* (*Niddah* 66b).

will be going to the *mikveh*, it is better (and easier) to avoid wearing waterproof mascara and other types of makeup that are difficult to remove.

After removing all make-up and contact lenses,[39] clean all mucous — dry or wet — from the outside and inside of your eyes. If you find wet mucous on the inside of your eyes after your *tevilah*, it does not invalidate your immersion.[40]

Nose

Clean any mucous from the inside of your nose. If you have a constantly runny nose (from allergies or the like), the mucous is not a *chatzitzah* — just blow your nose as best as you can before you immerse.

Teeth

Brush and floss your teeth well. If flossing makes your gums bleed, it poses no problems for your *tevilah*, as fresh blood from a wound is not a *chatzitzah*.[41] Simply rinse your mouth as best as you can.

After brushing and flossing your teeth, do not eat or drink anything except water. (Make sure you don't forget to eat and drink adequately before you complete this step, so that you don't feel faint by the time you get home from the *mikveh!*)

On the day of your immersion, it is prohibited to eat meat or chicken, since particles of these foods can sometimes be difficult to remove. If your *mikveh* night falls on *motzaei Shabbos* or *motzaei Yom Tov*, or on a day when you are attending a *seudas mitzvah* (a meal accompanying a *bris*, *pidyon haben* or *siyum*, for example) you are allowed to eat these foods that day.[42]

If you have dentures, remove them before immersing.[43]

---

39 See *Igros Moshe Yoreh Deah* I:104 and *Shiurei Shevet HaLevi* 198:7:2, who both state that if a woman forgot to remove her contact lenses she does not need to immerse again.

40 *Yoreh Deah* 198:7.

41 *Yoreh Deah* 198:9. Further, the *halachah* against swallowing human blood only applies after it has left your body.

42 *Yoreh Deah* 198:24 and *Taz* ad loc.

43 A woman who wears dentures and forgot to remove them must consult a *halachic* authority.

According to most *halachic* authorities, braces are not a *chatzitzah*;[44] they simply need to be cleaned very well.

Hair

Since it's best to save your final shower until you arrive at the *mikveh*, it's easier to wash your hair at that time. However, if you prefer to do this at home, then either during your bath or afterwards in the shower, shampoo your hair.[45]

You may use conditioner, as it is not considered a *chatzitzah*.[46] However, make sure it is rinsed out well.

Your hair needs to be combed while wet.[47] Some women find it easier to comb out their hair while under the shower, while others prefer to do this afterwards. If you comb out your hair after your shower, lay a towel over your shoulders to minimize stray hairs sticking to your body. After you have washed and combed out your hair, any remaining dandruff is not a *chatzitzah*.[48]

After you have finished combing out your hair, run your hands over your entire body to remove any stray hairs.

Permanent hair dyes (dyes that are not designed to continually wash out) are not considered a *chatzitzah*.[49] If a dye has started to wear out or your natural color can be seen at the roots, it is also not a *chatzitzah*, since most observant women do not mind this (because they cover their hair anyway). But if the roots bother you

---

[44] *Igros Moshe Yoreh Deah* 1:97 is stricter. He rules this way, but only in a case where water can get between the teeth and the braces.

[45] If you are preparing at home, re-comb your hair when you arrive at the *mikveh*, unless it is *Shabbos* or *Yom Tov*.

[46] *Mareh Kohen* pg.96 ftn. 42. Moreover, chemically, hair conditioners (those that are designed to be rinsed out) consist of two molecules which coat the hair. *Halachah* does not consider these two molecules significant; therefore, their presence does not count as a *chatzitzah*. (See Rashba in *Toras HaBayis*, end of 7:7, regarding the principle of *mamashis* that states that something that doesn't have any "substance," is not visual and is used for beauty is not a *chatzitzah*.)

[47] *Chochmas Adam* 120:2.

[48] See *Shiurei Shevet HaLevi* 198:22:4, where he says to wash the hair well and remove what is practical, but what is left is not a problem.

[49] *Shiurei Shevet HaLevi* 198:17.

personally, they become a *chatzitzah* for you, and you either need to remove all the dye or re-dye your hair before you immerse.[50]

If you have dyed your hair with a non-permanent dye — one that is designed to rinse out — you need to remove the dye only if you notice it coming out while you are preparing for the *mikveh*.[51]

Cutting Your Hair and Shaving Your Legs

Even if your hair needs cutting, it is not considered a *chatzitzah* if you don't cut it before you immerse.[52] However, if you plan to cut it, do so at least a day before your *tevilah*, so that any stray hairs do not get stuck in the crevices of your body. Similarly, you do not need to shave your legs before your *tevilah*, unless you are personally particular about having your legs shaved. In this case, you will need to shave your legs before *tevilah*. It is better to shave your legs the day before you immerse; however, you may shave on the day of your *tevilah*. Waxing needs to be done the day before.

Scabs

A scab that is still attached to your body and therefore a necessary part of the healing process is not a *chatzitzah*; it's healing skin. However, a scab that is ready to come off is dead skin that is no longer needed and is a *chatzitzah*.

The best way to tell the difference is to try gently to remove the scab after soaking. If it's ready to come off, it will do so easily without bleeding. Sometimes only a part of a scab is ready to come off, leaving little pieces at the edge. These pieces are not considered a *chatzitzah*. A scab that is still attached should be softened before your immersion.[53]

---

[50] As heard from Rav Yitzchak Berkovits.
[51] *Shiurei Shevet HaLevi* 198:17.
[52] See *Igros Moshe Yoreh Deah* 2:80 and also *Shu't Shevet HaLevi* 4:109.
[53] *Yoreh Deah* 198:9.

Calluses

Some *halachic* authorities rule that a callus is never a *chatzitzah*. Others rule that if a callus is large and bothersome, it must be removed to the point where it is small and not bothersome.[54]

Peeling Skin

Peeling skin — for example, from sunburn — is not a *chatzitzah*, since most women are not bothered by this. Any peeling skin that is loose after your bath and shower should be removed *gently* as best as possible.[55] A woman that personally minds the peeling skin that is left will need to get rid of it, since for her, it is a *chatzitzah*.

Blood From a Fresh Wound

Fresh blood coming out of a wound is not a *chatzitzah*, but congealed or dried blood is and needs to be removed.[56]

Mucous

If you have a constantly runny nose (from allergies or the like), the mucous is not a *chatzitzah*; just blow your nose as best as you can right before you immerse.

Stains on the Skin

Stains on your skin should be removed as best as possible before you immerse in the *mikveh*. Particularly tough stains may need lemon juice, vinegar or even a little bleach (diluted in water) to remove. If it is not possible to remove a stain, it is not a *chatzitzah* if it has no "thickness," for example, a pen mark, a beet or carrot stain, or the like. Thus, it is possible to immerse with these types of stains.[57]

---

[54] *Shiurei Shevet HaLevi* 198:22:4 and *Badei HaShulchan* 198:165. *Shiurei Shevet HaLevi* rules that, with the exception of long nails and possibly hair, parts of the body are never considered a *chatzitzah*, since they are the body itself. He also quotes the disputing opinion.

[55] *Shiurei Shevet HaLevi* 198:22:4.

[56] *Yoreh Deah* 198:9.

[57] *Shiurei Shevet HaLevi* 198:17.

Lice and Nits

The best way to remove lice is to use a comb specially designed for this purpose. If you suspect that you have lice, wash and condition your hair and comb thoroughly with a lice comb. After each stroke, wipe the comb on a white or light-colored tissue. You may need to look at the tissue with a magnifying glass. (Many of the better lice combs contain a magnifying glass in them.) Keep combing until the tissue is free from any lice. Then rinse your hair well. After this process, any lice or remaining eggs (nits) that you may inadvertently have missed are not considered a *chatzitzah*.[58]

If you live in an area where lice is a problem (usually among children of grade-school age), keep a lice comb on hand, so that if you suspect you may have lice, you have a method of removing them before your *mikveh* night.

Blisters, Pimples, Etc.

Closed or even open blisters, pimples and the like are not a *chatzitzah*. Closed blisters, pimples, etc. do not need to be opened, just washed well.[59]

Splinters

A splinter that is visible above the skin is a *chatzitzah* and needs to be removed before immersion. A splinter that is completely embedded under the skin is not a *chatzitzah*.[60]

Problems That May Prevent Going to the Mikveh on Time

Always consult a *halachic* authority if you think there is some part of your

---

[58] There is a question among *halachic* authorities whether lice is a *chatzitzah* or not. The *Shulchan Aruch* (*Yoreh Deah* 198:47) rules that lice are a *chatzitzah*, however, it seems that the lice that are described in the *Shulchan Aruch* are not the type that we have today. (See *Badei HaShulchan* 198:353, who appears to rule that our lice are not a *chatzitzah*, unless the woman herself is concerned.) However, *Shiurei Shevet HaLevi* 198:47 assumes that the ruling of *Shulchan Aruch* applies to today's lice.

[59] *Badei HaShulchan* 198:165.

[60] *Yoreh Deah* 198:11.

body that the waters of the *mikveh* would be unable to reach. Don't just assume that you may not immerse. Specifically, the following are areas of concern:

Stitches

Internal stitches (the type that are made to dissolve) are usually not a *chatzitzah*; exterior stitches can be a *chatzitzah* and can prevent going to the *mikveh*.[61] If you have stitches or know that you will need stitches at a time that you will be going to the *mikveh*, consult a *halachic* authority beforehand.

Casts

A cast on a part of the body is usually a *chatzitzah*. If you have a cast, consult a *halachic* authority.

Temporary Dental Work

Temporary dental work may be a *chatzitzah*. If you are in the middle of dental work (or need to schedule it), consult a *halachic* authority.

---

[61] *Shiurei Shevet HaLevi* 198:11:3 and *Badei HaShulchan* 198:23 *Biurim* s.v. Bi'eged. *Badei HaShulchan* notes, however, that often stitches are not so tight and water can get underneath them; thus they would not necessarily be a *chatzitzah*.

CHAPTER 8

♦

Immersing in the Mikveh

A typical *mikveh* looks like a small, sunken pool. Stairs lead down to the water, which is normally chest-level,[1] warm and clean. The *mikveh* is usually either in a room connected to a preparation room — a place where you can get ready for your immersion — or inside the preparation room itself.

Many *mikveh* houses provide you with all the amenities you need to do your *chafifah* (cleansing) in advance of immersion — soap, shampoo, combs, dental floss, scissors, towels and toothbrushes (new, of course!).

Private preparation rooms normally include a bathtub, shower, sink and toilet, as well as a place to hang your clothes. Some are the size of a normal bathroom, others quite spacious and luxurious. There is usually a separate room with hair dryers and big mirrors for your use after your *tevilah*. The fee for using the *mikveh* generally varies according to the amenities you use.

As we discussed in Chapter 5, it is an individual decision whether to prepare for your *tevilah* at home or at the *mikveh*.[2] Some women are more comfortable in their own surroundings, while others enjoy a relaxing break from the hectic atmosphere at home.

---

[1]   *Yoreh Deah* 198:36.
[2]   Although as noted in Ch. 5, some authorities say it is *halachically* preferable to prepare at the *mikveh*.

If you decide to prepare at home, it is recommended to take a short shower at the *mikveh* when you arrive;[3] also, it's best to save the final comb-out of your hair until just before immersion (with the exception of *Shabbos* or *Yom Tov*, if you arrive at the *mikveh* after sunset).

When you arrive at the *mikveh*, an attendant will greet you, show you to your preparation room and make sure it is clean. She will also let you know how to contact her when you've finished preparing and are ready to immerse. In some neighborhoods, you may have to wait for a preparation room on a busy night.

In some communities, it is necessary to call the *mikveh* attendant ahead of time and make an appointment. Even in larger communities, this may be necessary if your *mikveh* night falls on *Shabbos* or a *Yom Tov*. If you are planning on using a *mikveh* away from home, it's always a good idea to make inquiries beforehand as to what the procedure is in the community where you will be a guest.

The Time of Immersion

The first possible time you may immerse is at nightfall after your Seven Clean Days have finished. Your *mikveh* night will always fall out on the same day of the week as your *hefsek taharah*. For example, if you made your *hefsek* on a Tuesday afternoon, then you will go to the *mikveh* the following Tuesday night.

Barring extenuating circumstances (which we will discuss below), you should not delay your night of immersion. It is a *mitzvah* to go to the *mikveh* on time.[4]

Some *mikveh* houses open close to sunset so that you can immerse at the first possible time; others open at a specific hour, which can change depending on the season.

If you are in a place where it could be dangerous to go to the *mikveh* at night, consult a *halachic* authority.[5]

---

[3]   Especially if there has been a time lapse between doing your *chafifah* and arriving at the *mikveh*.

[4]   *Yoreh Deah* 197:2.

[5]   It is usually possible in such a case to make arrangements to use the *mikveh* during the daytime on the eighth day (after the Seven Clean Days have finished). In addition, there are

The Mitzvah of Iyun

Torah law requires that you inspect yourself thoroughly before you immerse to make sure that there is nothing adhering to your body that would render your immersion invalid.[6] This final inspection is called iyun. A tevilah without iyun is invalid.[7]

After finishing all your preparations, do a preliminary iyun yourself before you call the mikveh attendant. It is especially helpful to run your hands over your entire body to remove any stray hairs that you were unable to see.

The mikveh attendant should do iyun with you another time just before your tevilah.[8] Although you can do iyun entirely by yourself, this is the ideal way to fulfill this commandment.

Verification is also needed to assure that your entire body, including your hair, is immersed at the same time.[9] This is done by an observant Jewish woman over the age of 12, normally your mikveh attendant.[10] In an emergency (a case where no one else is around), your husband can verify your immersion.[11] If no one is available, you may immerse by yourself with a loose hairnet or something similar that will make sure that all your hair is pulled under the water.[12]

How to Immerse

When you enter the water of the mikveh, you will find the water about chest

---

halachic authorities who permit a woman to go to the mikveh on the seventh day under certain extenuating circumstances.

6   Bava Kama 82a.
7   Ibid.
8   Yoreh Deah 198:40.
9   Yoreh Deah 198:40.
10   Ibid.
11   See Shu't Noda BiYehudah, Yoreh Deah 2:122, who explains that although a husband is not permitted to see certain parts of his wife's body while she is niddah (and she is niddah until she immerses), this is because of the concern that he will come to do an aveirah. Since she will be immersing in a matter of seconds, he is permitted to see these parts (and can even help her with the mitzvah of iyun).
12   Yoreh Deah 198:40.

high. An easy way to assure that your entire body and all your hair are completely under the water is to first spring up a little bit with your feet so that the force of gravity helps pull you down. As you go under the water, bend your knees slightly. You do not need to lift your feet off the floor of the *mikveh* when you immerse.[13]

Even though the water of the *mikveh* needs to reach all parts of your body that are naturally exposed, you don't need to open your mouth or eyes.[14] However, you do need to keep these parts, as well as your hands and the rest of your body, relaxed. If, for some reason a woman needs support to immerse, she may loosely hold on to a railing or to someone else's hand under water.[15]

A woman is not allowed to immerse in a rushed manner or in a place that isn't completely private (which may cause her to rush).[16]

Different Customs of Immersion

There are many different customs regarding the number of times to immerse, even though once is enough to change your spiritual status.[17] Most women immerse at least twice; some three times or even more.[18]

The reason for immersing two times is based upon a dispute among *halachic* authorities: For most *mitzvos*, we make the blessing before doing the *mitzvah*. However, in a few specific instances, we make the blessing after doing the *mitzvah*, since there are certain situations that preclude the blessing being said beforehand.

For example, we make the blessing *Al Netilas Yadayim* after the hands have been washed. This is because there is a time when this blessing cannot be said

---

13   *Yoreh Deah* 198:30.
14   *Yoreh Deah* 198:35–39.
15   *Badei HaShulchan* 198:217.
16   *Yoreh Deah* 198:34.
17   *Yoreh Deah* 200:1.
18   Two times is mentioned by *Shelah* (cited by *Ba'er Heitev, Yoreh Deah* 200:1) and *Shu't Chavos Yair* 181. *Sefer Chassidim* 394 mentions three times, based on the fact that Yechezkel 36:25 mentions *taharah* three times.

before the washing (for example, in the morning or after using the bathroom, since the hands need to be washed first before the blessing can be said).

Similarly, a convert cannot make the required blessing before immersing, since he or she is not yet Jewish. Thus, it is made after immersing. Some *halachic* authorities contend that the blessing on *tevilah* is recited afterwards because of the time when it cannot be said before.[19]

Others disagree,[20] and thus, we are left with a dispute among *halachic* authorities as to when the best time for a woman to recite the blessing on *tevilah* is — before or after the immersion.

Sefardi women follow the opinion which says the blessing is made before immersing.[21] The common custom among *Ashkenazi* women is to immerse two times and make the blessing in between the two immersions.

Practical Procedure for Ashkenazi Women

The procedure for immersion for *Ashkenazi* women is as follows: Hand your towel to the *mikveh* attendant and walk down the stairs to the *mikveh*. When you are ready, immerse. The attendant will let you know that your immersion was complete by saying, "kosher." She will then hand you either a towel or a scarf with which to cover your hair before you make the blessing. (The rest of your body is covered by the water.)

Next, make the following blessing:

> *Baruch Atah Adonoy Eloheinu Melech ha-olam, Asher kidshanu b'mitzvosav v'tzivanu al ha-tevilah.*

This blessing is usually posted on the wall of the *mikveh*, so that you can see it from the water. If you need help with the blessing, ask your attendant. Place your arm under your chest (right above the waist) to make a separation between the

---

19 Rama, *Yoreh Deah* 200:1.
20 *Yoreh Deah* 200:1.
21 And not while standing in the *mikveh*.

upper and lower half of your body while making the blessing.[22] After you've said the blessing, hand your head covering back to the attendant and immerse again.

Many women have the custom to then say a prayer regarding the rebuilding of the Temple in Jerusalem, followed by private prayers.[23] After saying these prayers, some women immerse again.

After Immersion

Because of the seriousness of the laws of *tevilah*, we are very particular in our preparations. However, afterwards, we are advised not to worry or have anxiety that we might have forgotten something.[24]

Yet, if right after your *tevilah*, you find that you have indeed overlooked something, you should immerse again. If you are uncertain about something, consult a *halachic* authority, even if you have already gone home.

After your *tevilah*, the accepted practice is not to bathe or shower at the *mikveh*.[25]

---

22 See *Taz* 200:3; *Shach* 200:1; and *Shiurei Shevet HaLevi* 200:9.

23 The prayer reads, "May it be your will, *Adonoy*, our God and God of our forefathers, that the Holy Temple be rebuilt, speedily in our days. Grant us our share in your *Torah*, and may we serve you there in reverence, as in days of old and in former years. Then the offering of Judah and Jerusalem will be pleasing to *Adonoy*, as in days of old and in former years." This is the prayer that is said during daily davening after the *Amidah*. Some *halachic* authorities say that *Hashem*'s name is omitted when reciting this prayer in the *mikveh* (*Shiurei Shevet HaLevi* 200:1:8). It is customary to say this prayer after doing a *mitzvah* whose observance is affected by the *Churban*, the destruction of the Temple. Since the *Churban*, women only immerse in a *mikveh* for family reasons, whereas *mikveh* observance should also be associated with eating and handling *terumah* and *kodoshim* and entering the Holy Temple. For a similar reason, some women say this prayer after taking *challah*.

24 Ramban in *Sidrei Taharah* 198:55; see also Rambam in *Hilchos Niddah* 9:25.

25 Rama, *Yoreh Deah* 201:75. *Sefardim* do not have this custom (see *Birkei Yosef Yoreh Deah* 201:25; *Shu't Yabia Omer* 8: *Yoreh Deah*: 19). The origin of this custom is as follows: A *takana*, or rabbinic ban (instituted for the purpose of making a "spiritual repair") was made (see *Zavim* 5:12 and *Shabbos* 13b) that someone who bathes or showers in water not kosher for a *mikveh* becomes *tamei* (*miderabanan*, rabbinically). The *Gemara* (*Shabbos* 14a) records the following historical background to this custom: At the time of the *Gemara*, kosher *mikvaos* were often natural springs that were not necessarily very clean. After *tevilah*, people would bathe in order to clean themselves. Hence, there was a concern that people would begin to think that

Leaving the Mikveh

Our *halachic* sources state that if the first thing a woman sees upon leaving the *mikveh* is a *davar tamei*, a non-kosher animal, this affects a child conceived that night.[26] To prevent such an occurrence, one "meets" the *mikveh* attendant first by seeing and touching her (for example, shaking her hand).[27]

Arriving at Home

Even though it is most likely that your husband is aware that you've just been to the *mikveh*, there is a *halachic* requirement that, upon returning, you inform him verbally that you have immersed.[28]

---

it was the bath that made them *tahor* and not the *tevilah*, falsely believing that immersing in the *mikveh* was unnecessary. Therefore, the Sages made a *gezeirah* (decree) that after immersing in a bath, a person could not eat *terumah*.

Most opinions contend that this *takanah* was established only to invalidate someone from eating *terumah*, however, Rama, *Yoreh Deah* 201:75 quotes the *Mordechai* (a book written by a *rishon* who lived in Germany in the 13th century), who cites a minority opinion that contends that this *takanah* also applies to a *niddah* after *tevilah* (meaning, a woman may not bathe in water not kosher for *mikveh* use after *tevilah* so that she would not come to say that it was the bath that made her *tahor* and not the *mikveh*). Rama (Ibid) records this as the accepted custom. However, neither the *Mordechai* nor Rama record for how long a woman should wait before bathing.

Shu't Shevet HaLevi 5:125 says that once a woman touches her husband, or her husband touches her, this demonstrates that the *mikveh* is what removes the *tumah*, she is permitted to bathe or shower. *Lechem VeSimlah* 201:222 rules that even those who rule that she should not bathe agree that she may shower. *Marei Kohen* (Ch. 6 ftn. 109) quotes from Rav Shlomo Zalman Auerbach that she may shower upon returning home, but should not shower or bathe at the *mikveh*, nor should she bathe at home. *Shu't Tzitz Eliezer* 11:64:10 quotes several sources that permit her to shower at the *mikveh*, as long she does not wash both her body and her hair at the same time, and bathe at home.

26 Rama, *Yoreh Deah* 198:48. The sources of Rama are the early *Ashkenazi halachic* authorities (the *Shaarei Dura, Rokeach, Kolbo, Maharil*).

27 *Sidrei Taharah* 198:91 (See also *Shearim HaMetzuyanim BaHalachah* 162:11, who quote *Shu't Pri HaSadeh* 4:145, where he says that it is only a problem if she confronts a *tamei* species of animal, but not if the *mikveh* attendant herself is *temeiah* (*niddah*).

28 *Yoreh Deah* 185:1 (based on *Niddah* 11b). *Chavos Daas* there (quoted by *Pischei Teshuvah*) assumes the *Shulchan Aruch* means that she must verbally state that she immersed. Other *halachic*

Tevilah on Shabbos and Yom Tov

If your *mikveh* night falls on a *Shabbos* or *Yom Tov* — even if it falls on a *Shabbos* that follows a two-day *Yom Tov* — you should go to the *mikveh* on time. Review the *halachos* of *chatzitzah* (see Ch. 5) so your immersion can be anxiety-free.

The procedure for the actual *tevilah* on *Shabbos* and *Yom Tov* is the same as that for a weekday. However, after immersing you must be careful not to violate the prohibitions of the day; for example, you may not squeeze water out of your hair or towel.

When you come out of the *mikveh*, dab the towel over your hair to dry it. When your hair is somewhat dry to the touch, you may lightly run your hands through it or touch it up with a special, soft *Shabbos* brush.

You will also need to be careful when you are drying yourself not to let the towel become so wet that water is squeezed out of it. It helps to run your fingers over your body to get rid of excess water before using your towel.

You may apply a liquid or spray perfume or deodorant to your body on *Shabbos* or *Yom Tov*, but not to your clothing.[29] Oil or a liquid moisturizer may be applied to your skin to maintain it in the condition it was at the beginning of *Shabbos*.[30]

Keeping Your Mikveh Night Private

The night you go to the *mikveh* should be kept private.[31] However, other people are allowed to know if this knowledge is necessary to facilitate your *tevilah*.[32]

---

authorities accept the disputing opinion of *Lechem VeSimlah* 185:1 and *Aruch HaShulchan* 185:4, who contend that *Shulchan Aruch* did not mean that she must verbally tell her husband that she went to the *mikveh*, but that it is sufficient if she does something that shows her husband that she immersed. The prevalent custom is that a woman tells her husband verbally that she has immersed.

29 *Mishnah Berurah* 322:18.

30 *Orach Chayim* 327:1. This is different from applying oil or a liquid moisturizer for healing purposes, which is not allowed on *Shabbos*.

31 Rama, *Yoreh Deah* 198:48. This *halachah* is based on an interpretation of a *Gemara* in *Eruvin* 55b.

32 *Badei HaShulchan* 198:371 and footnotes.

In a case where others (including family members) will realize where you are going, you do not need to be concerned and should not postpone your *tevilah*.[33]

Tevilah When Your Husband Is Out of Town and Other Circumstances

The following circumstances apply only in cases where the Seven Clean Days have been completed:

If your husband will not be in town on your *mikveh* night, you do not need to go to the *mikveh*. Moreover, many *halachic* authorities contend that it is better for a woman not to go to the *mikveh* in this circumstance.[34]

If your husband will be returning during the daytime, you should go to the *mikveh* the night before.[35] Similarly, if you are returning from a trip after the *mikveh* will be closed (or if one of you is returning on a Friday, and it is difficult to go to the *mikveh* that night), you should immerse the night before. However, during the night (or nights) that you spend without your husband after you have immersed, it is recommended that you sleep with a knife under your pillow.[36]

If, on your *mikveh* night, you and your husband anticipate being in different towns, but there is a chance that you will be together, you should go to the *mikveh* on time.[37]

---

[33] See also *Badei HaShulchan* 198:24 *biurim "uminhag"*, quoting *Shu't Beis Shearim* 280. In a case when the public will know, see *Shiurei Shevet HaLevi* 197:2:13 on *Shach* 3, who quotes *Shu't Yehuda Yaaleh, Yoreh Deah* 217. *Yehuda Yaaleh* rules that a woman is permitted to postpone her *tevilah* until Friday night if otherwise the public will know when she went to *mikveh*. The case he quotes involves a woman who operates a store that is open until late at night and her only way to immerse during the week is to close the store, thus advertising the fact that she went to the *mikveh*.

[34] See *Shu't Shvus Yaakov* 3:77, who considers that a woman going to the *mikveh* in such a circumstance places herself in danger of attack from a *dibbuk*, a "wandering soul" that can possess the body of a human being.

[35] *Shiurei Shevet HaLevi* 197:2; however, he notes that there are some *halachic* authorities who disagree with him.

[36] See also *Shu't Shvus Yaakov* 3:77, who also suggests having a child sleep in the wife's bed with her. Some suggest her taking a garment of her husbands to bed with her, such as his pajamas.

[37] *Shiurei Shevet HaLevi* 197:2:1.

You may go to the *mikveh*, even if you and your husband are unable to have marital relations, even if your night of *tevilah* falls on *Shabbos* or a *Yom Tov*.[38]

Tevilah During Shivah

If a woman is sitting *shivah*, she may not go to *mikveh* until the *shivah* is over.[39] If the husband is sitting *shivah* and his wife's scheduled time to go to the *mikveh* falls during that week, there is a disagreement among *halachic* authorities as to whether or not his wife should go to *mikveh* at the correct time or wait until his *shivah* is over.[40] In this case, the couple should consult their *halachic* authority.

---

[38] *Badei HaShulchan* 197:2 *biurim*.

[39] *Yoreh Deah* 381:5.

[40] *Badei HaShulchan* 197:16 quotes this dispute between *poskim*. Those who feel the wife should wait until the end of her husband's period of mourning is over are concerned that he will have relations with her even though he is not permitted (see *Shu't Maharam Shick* 365). *Pischei Teshuvah* 197:8 rules that a wife may immerse during her husband's period of mourning.

♦

CHAPTER 9

Togetherness

In this chapter, we will first discuss the Jewish perspective of physicality and then marital intimacy. Afterwards, the laws governing marital relations are presented. Because the Jewish perspective on these subjects differs so dramatically from the non-Jewish world, an understanding of our Jewish view is crucial to being able to keep the laws properly.

We will see that the laws reflect the type of loving relationship our Sages speak of between husband and wife, as well as give us a way to create ever-increasing levels of harmony, intimacy and joy.

The Physical as a Pathway to the Spiritual

In Judaism, the physical world is not disdained. On the contrary, because we are both physical and spiritual beings — made this way purposely by our Creator — we are specifically required not to ignore this dimension of our existence. Rather, we are encouraged to use it to reach our spiritual goals, namely, to improve ourselves as people and grow closer to our Creator.

Indeed, disdaining the physical world as a goal in itself is not looked upon favorably in Judaism. Our spiritual leaders are required to marry, as are all men; similarly, they (and we) do not take vows of silence for long periods of time, or follow other practices that attempt to promote a path to the spiritual through the denial of the physical.

The *Gemara* teaches us, "Shmuel said, 'Whoever fasts [for the sake of self-affliction] is called a sinner.' He is of the same opinion as the *Tanna*[1] Rabbi Elazar HaKappar Berabbi [who taught] 'What is the *Torah* referring to when it says[2] [of the *nazir*[3]], "And [the *Kohen*] will make atonement for him,[4] since he sinned against the soul." Against which soul did he sin? [This must refer to the fact that] he denied himself wine. Now, how much more so: If this man [the *nazir*] who denied himself only wine is called a sinner, how much more so he who distresses himself by abstaining from all [permitted] things [is considered a sinner]?' "[5]

The primary reason why Judaism prohibits unnecessary abstention from physicality is because partaking of the physical world in the prescribed way *maximizes* our spiritual growth.

Let us begin to illustrate this point by a simple example. Everyone who has ever tried to diet knows that it's far easier to simply fast than to cut down on one's food intake and make life-long, healthy changes in one's dietary habits. Everyone also knows that fasting may take off weight in the short term, but it's not a viable option for the long term!

Similarly, using — in the correct manner — the permissible pleasures that God in His goodness has given us leads to much greater spiritual growth than would result from simply abstaining from them.

This idea is eloquently expressed by Rav Shimshon Raphael Hirsch, who writes,

> *The spirit of Judaism knows of no cleavage in human existence which assigns the spirit of man to God and his body to Satan ... "Prepare for Me here on earth a holy abode, so I may dwell with you already here on earth," says the spirit of*

---

[1] A *Tanna* is one of our Sages whose teachings about the Oral Law were written down in the *Mishnah*.

[2] *Bamidbar* 6:11.

[3] Someone who has taken a type of vow that requires him or her to abstain from wine for a specific period of time.

[4] After the period of his vow ends, the *nazir* is required to bring an atonement offering to the *Beis HaMikdash*.

[5] *Ta'anis* 11a.

Judaism in the name of God. It takes the whole being of man, both sensual and spiritual, into its domain, so that even sensuous enjoyment becomes a holy serv-ice of God when it is inspired with the spirit of modesty, temperance and holi-ness, and when man enjoys the goods and gifts and attractions of the earth in a manner so pure and acceptable to God and for such holy and acceptable ends that he can raise his eyes cheerfully and joyfully to God and does not need to flee from the neighborhood of His sanctuary. To be able to abide in the sphere of God even with his physical satisfaction and enjoyments - this is the highest perfection of the morally endowed man upon earth.[6]

Fostering a partnership between the spiritual and physical in a way that uses the physical as a springboard to the spiritual is a lifetime project. Although these two aspects of our being often seem to be at odds with each other, it is our chal-lenge to elevate the physical to serve the spiritual. It is precisely through meeting this challenge that we grow, both in our own character development and in close-ness to our Creator.

How is this process accomplished? Indeed, this task would be daunting if not for the guidelines our Creator Himself gives us in the form of His *Torah* and its *mitzvos*. Our first and very important step is to meticulously make use of the in-formation He gives us.

Simply following our Creator's instructions gives us the power to transform the physical and make it work for use in the spiritual realm. For example, regard-ing *Shabbos*, we are instructed to delight in it and honor it.[7] The Rambam[8] tells us that we honor *Shabbos* through our preparations in the physical world — clean-ing the house, making special food, wearing one's best clothing and the like. The delight of *Shabbos* comes on the day itself, for example, through savoring this spe-cial food we have prepared. In turn, it is this delight that fosters our connection to our Creator on this special day.

For those who have spent part of their lives not keeping *Shabbos* and only later

---

[6]   Shimshon Raphael Hirsch, Collected Writings, Vol. 2, pp. 320–321.
[7]   *Yeshayahu* 58:13–14.
[8]   *Hilchos Shabbos* 30:2,3,7.

as adults took on this *mitzvah*, one may ask, how can it be that previously, Saturdays came and went with no awareness of the special spiritual quality of this day, whereas now "Saturday" has been transformed into *Shabbos*? Simply by taking action in the physical world with the proper intentions opens our "spiritual conduits."

The *Torah* says, "You should be happy in your holiday."[9] We are then told by our Oral Tradition specific activities that stimulate our happiness. For men, the *Gemara* suggests drinking wine and eating meat, and for women, wearing new clothes.[10]

Partaking of (the permissible) physical pleasures stimulates our spiritual awareness through gladdening our hearts and uplifting our spirits. This, in turn, ultimately leads us to spiritual connection and growth. Moreover, it is only by experiencing happiness and pleasure in this world that we can reach the ultimate of spiritual heights.

Let us consider an example from the times when the Jewish people still had prophets. To receive Divine inspiration, the prophet had to be in a pleasant, joyous mood. A prophet who was depressed or angry was denied access to the Divine.[11] Specifically, the use of music is mentioned as a way of elevating a prophet's mood.[12]

For the same reason, when Yitzchak was preparing himself to bless his son Esau, a blessing that was to be accomplished through a prophetic vision, he asked Esau to "prepare tasty food that I desire so that I may eat and my soul will bless you."[13]

Even on one of the most serious days of the Jewish year, *Rosh Hashanah* — the Day of Judgment — we are especially particular to partake of physical pleasures (wearing holiday clothing, eating particularly tasty and sweet foods) as we have been instructed:

---

[9]   *Devarim* 16:14.
[10] *Pesachim* 109a.
[11] *Shabbos* 30b; *Pesachim* 117a.
[12] *Melachim II* 3:15.
[13] *Bereishis* 27:4.

This day is holy to Hashem your God; do not mourn or weep. For all the people wept when they heard the words of the Torah. Then he [Nechemiah] said to them, go your way, eat sumptuously and drink sweet beverages, and send portions to those for whom nothing is prepared: for this day is holy to Hashem: For the joy of Hashem is your strength.[14]

Even though *Shabbos* and our holidays carry with them special spiritual energy, this model is applicable to all our physical pursuits, on every day of the week.

Coming Close to God

One of the first steps we can take, on an everyday basis, to use the physical as a means to the spiritual is simply to appreciate the physical pleasure that God gives us. By turning our gratitude towards the Source of all our pleasure, we not only begin the process of elevating these pleasures, but also give ourselves an opportunity to connect to our Creator through appreciation of what He gives us. Through this process and connection to God, we grow spiritually.

The *Torah* tells us that failure to acknowledge our gratitude brings us dire consequences. Before Moshe *Rabbeinu* (Moses, our teacher) died, he admonished the Jewish people to keep God's commandments and enumerated the curses that would befall them if they failed to do so. However, he was particular to explain to them that the reason these curses would come about, saying they would be "as signs and proofs against you and your offspring forever, because you did not serve *Hashem*, your God, amid gladness and goodness of heart, when everything was abundant."[15] This tells us that when we are enjoying the goodness that God gives us, we are fully expected to acknowledge the source of these pleasures.

---

[14]   *Nechemiah* 8:9–10.
[15]   *Devarim* 28:47.

Actualizing Our Potential

It is clear that Judaism views physical pleasure not as an end in itself, but rather as a means given to us by God to actualize our spiritual potential — through becoming close to God and learning to emulate His ways.

The Power of Intimacy

We know that all permissible pleasures — pleasures through which we have the potential to become close to God and grow spiritually — carry an equal potential for the desecration of God's name: The greater the potential for holiness, the greater the possibility for desecration. Judaism teaches that physical intimacy between a man and woman has more potential than any other activity in the physical world in this regard. One reason is that it is more powerful.

The fact that we, as human beings, have free will is one of the best expressions of the *tzelem Elohim*, the image of God within us. Nowhere is the exercise of our free choice more pronounced than in the realm of intimacy. Here, we are offered the ultimate choice between the holy and the profane. One can take a path to the highest of spiritual highs or bring oneself down to the lowest point possible.

Intimacy is the instrument that can bring down a new soul from the spiritual world and create a living being; in this sense, it is the ultimate in giving. Profaned, it can be used to perpetrate some of the world's worst horrors.

The location of the Jewish people's covenant made with God, *bris milah*, underscores the choice to be made — between the ultimate in holiness or its diametric opposite. For here lies the greatest amount of free will available in the world: A man's choice is how he uses this part of his being. *Bris milah* comes to tell a man that the path to self-perfection comes through learning to control himself in his physical relations. From this, all other forms of self-perfection follow.[16]

---

[16]   The concepts in this section were heard from Rav Yitzchak Berkovits. See also Hirsch's Commentary to *Bereishis* 17:10 s.v. *areil basar*.

From Our Sages

Our Sages tell us:

- *Know, my children, that there is no holiness of all types of holiness comparable to the holiness of marital intimacy if a person sanctifies himself in marital relations in accordance with the instructions of our Sages.[17]*

- *Marital relations are an action that is important, good and valuable to the soul also, and there is no act of flesh and blood that compares with it — if it is done with a pure intention, and a pure and clean mind; then it is called holy.[18]*

- *Proper marital intimacy is called "knowing" (Bereishis 4:1) for good reason. As it is said, "And Elkanah knew his wife Chanah" (Shmuel I 1:19). The secret reason for this is that when the drop of seed is drawn in holiness and purity, it comes from the source of wisdom and understanding, which is the brain. Understand, therefore, that unless it involved matters of great holiness, marital intimacy would not be called "knowing."[19]*

- *There are three partners in man: They are God, his father and his mother. (Niddah 31a) ...Is it possible there is something unseemly in that of which God is a partner? The union of man with his wife, when it is proper, is the mystery of the foundation of the world and its civilizations. This is the mystery of what the Sages said, "When a man unites with his wife in holiness, the Shechinah rests between them." (Sotah 17a.)[20]*

Reaching Holiness Through Marital Intimacy

The marriage relationship between a husband and wife serves as a model for

---

[17] *Shelah HaKodesh, Shaar HaOsiyos, Kuf.*
[18] *Mor U'Ketziyah, Orach Chayim 240.*
[19] Ramban, *Igeres HaKodesh*, Ch. 2.
[20] Ibid.

our relationship to God. Our Sages tell us, "All of the writings of the *Tanach* are holy, and *Shir HaShirim*, The Song of Songs, is the Holy of Holies."[21] The Song of Songs, a description of the love between a man and a woman, is understood to be a metaphor for the relationship of God to the Jewish people. It is through this metaphor that we learn how to relate to our Creator and how to draw close and connect with His Divine Presence — both as individuals and as a nation.

The *Gemara* tells us, "Whenever Israel came up [to the Temple in Jerusalem] on the Festival, the curtain [covering the Holy of Holies] would be removed for them and the *keruvim* (cherubs) were shown to them, their bodies joined together in an embrace. And [the priests] would address [the nation]: Look! You are beloved before God as the love between man and woman."[22]

Marital intimacy channels a couple's feelings for each other in a way that removes barriers they might have put up between them due to minor irritants. It opens up a direct path to the soul of the other person and allows each partner to connect with the other in a profound way and sense the oneness between them. It is this oneness, this unity, that draws down the *Shechinah*.[23]

> ✦ [The *Zohar* says] *When a man joins [in intimacy] with his wife, and his intention is to sanctify himself as he should, then he is complete, and together they are called "one without blemish."*[24]

The Path to Holiness

The development of the relationship between husband and wife is part of our lifetime task of spiritually developing ourselves, becoming one with one another

---

21   *Yadayim* 3:5.
22   *Yoma* 54a.
23   See *Sidur Beis Yaakov, Hanhagas Leil Shabbos*, 7:2:6, where Rav Yaakov Emden explains, "There is no (marital intimacy) without embracing and kissing preceding it. And there are two kinds of kissing: The first is before marital relations, where the purpose of kissing is that the man soothes the woman and arouses the love between them; the other kind is during the intimacy itself, where the purpose is to accomplish the two kinds of unions, the lower one and the supernal one together."
24   *Reishis Chachmah, Shaar HaKedushah*, beginning of Ch. 16.

and becoming the best human beings we can possibly be. Newlyweds who are just beginning their lives together have no storehouse of shared, intimate experiences from which they have bonded over the years and from which these intentions arise.

Similarly, those who have only begun to keep Jewish law in their adult lives may wonder how they can counteract the negative influences of the secular world of which they have been a part for so many years. Even those who have been *Torah* observant all their lives are unfortunately not immune from these negative influences. However, just as God, in His wisdom, has given us the ability to "feel" *Shabbos*, when previously it was only "Saturday," so, too, He has given us the Laws of Family Purity and the laws of marital relations which serve to infuse every aspect of our being with holiness.

Taking the required steps in the physical world to keep these *mitzvos* begins this lifelong process of directing every part of ourselves to the path of holiness.

Halachah and Holiness

The *halachos* prescribed by the *Torah* and our Sages help a couple focus on their love for one another, and thus point the way toward holiness. Far from being a killjoy of pleasure,[25] these *halachos* serve to increase each spouse's connection to the other by assuring that the soul is an equal partner with the body in intimate relations.

Halachic Obligations

A husband has a *Torah* obligation to please his wife and be intimate with her, both physically[26] and emotionally.[27] This is referred to as the *mitzvah* of *onah* (literally, the commandment of time). Indeed, to sanctify himself in holiness in marital

---

[25] After the revelation at Mount Sinai, God told Moses to tell the people, "Go say to them, return to your tents." (*Devarim* 5:27.) Commenting on this verse, the *Gemara* (*Avodah Zarah* 5a) tells us this refers to the joy of *onah* (marital relations had been forbidden for three days prior to the revelation).

[26] "He shall not diminish her conjugal rights." (*Shemos* 21:10.)

[27] See *Pesachim* 72b; *Orach Chayim* 240:1; *Yoreh Deah* 184:10.

relations, approaching relations with this intention is essential.[28] The *Gemara* mentions more than once that a reward is given to a man who pleases his wife before himself.[29]

In addition to being intimate with his wife on a regular basis, a husband's *mitzvah* of *onah* also includes pleasing his wife when "(he) sees that his wife desires to be intimate with him... (meaning) that he is required to please his wife when he sees that she desires him."[30]

To properly fulfill the *mitzvah* of *onah*, he must desire to please her and acquire an ability to respond to her and show her how much he cares about her.[31]

The *Gemara* says a wife should not request marital relations from her husband in a direct manner,[32] as doing so risks causing damage to herself, her husband and the soul of a child that might be conceived during this time.[33] (For more discussion of this concept, see the section below on *Special Considerations — The Nine Middos*.)

At the same time, our Sages enumerate the tremendous reward for a wife who shows her husband her desire to be intimate with him in an indirect manner, for example, through showing special affection to him or the like.

> *Rav Shmuel ben Nachmani said in the name of Rav Yochanan,* "Any woman who [indirectly] *solicits her husband to marital intimacy will have children the likes of whom did not exist even in the generation of Moshe.*" [34]

Both husband and wife have an obligation to be intimate with each other.[35]

---

28 Rambam, *Hilchos De'os* 3:2; *Orach Chayim* 240:1.
29 *Bava Basra* 10b; *Niddah* 31b.
30 See *Pesachim* 72b and *Igros Moshe Even HaEzer* 3:28.
31 See *Igros Moshe Even HaEzer* 1:102.
32 *Eruvin* 100b, *Nedarim* 20b.
33 Regarding damage to either or both of them, see Raavad in *Shaar HaKedushah*, quoted by *Beis Yosef* to 240. The concept of a "blemished soul" means that it has a lot of *yetzer harah* (evil inclination) and bad character traits that will require much work to repair. However, it is not predestined to be evil. Thus, correction of its *middos* (character traits) will be harder but very doable (see *Kehilos Yaakov Yevamos* 49 and *Igros Moshe Even HaEzer* 4:14). Studying *Torah* is mentioned as a method of *tikun* (correction).
34 *Eruvin* 100b.
35 See *Kesubos* 63a; *Nedarim* 15b and 81b.

Indeed, both *halachically* and practically, developing the ability to please one another is part of their mutual obligation to create and maintain *shalom bayis*, peace in the home. Just as a husband must understand his wife's desires to properly fulfill the *mitzvah* of *onah*, a wife is instructed to please her husband in any way that he desires.[36] If a couple has differences, they should feel free to discuss them with each other.

Parameters of Relations

Lighting

Halachah prohibits an open source of light in the room when a couple is in the act of having relations, regardless of how dim it might be. "Open source" means an electric light or candle without a shade.[37]

If a couple does desire some light, the light should come from outside the room or from a covered light in the room and should be dim enough that one cannot see too clearly.[38]

Relations at Night

The *Gemara* says that "Jews are holy and do not have relations in the daytime."[39] The *Gemara* then mentions an exception to the rule: It is permitted if the room is dark. Rav Moshe Feinstein explains that relations in the daytime are permitted only because this occurrence is not frequent or the circumstances are extenuating.[40]

---

[36] *Nedarim* 20b.

[37] Rama, *Orach Chayim* 240:11.

[38] *Shelah, Os Kuf* quoting *Seder HaYom*; *Sidur Beis Yaakov* (of Rav Yaakov Emden), *Hanhagas Leil Shabbos* 7:3:5 A number of reasons for this *halachah* are given in various sources: The *Gemara* (*Niddah* 17a) says it is so that the husband does not see something unpleasant in his wife. Rashi (to *Shabbos* 86a) says it is because of tzniyus. Rambam (*Hilchos Issurei Bi'ah* 21:10) says that it is brazen. *Shelah (Os Kuf)* quotes *Seder HaYom* saying that it is "dangerous" for their children. An item such as a digital display on a clock is not considered an open source of light (as heard by Rav Yitzchak Berkovits).

[39] *Shabbos* 86a; *Kesubos* 65b; *Niddah* 17a.

[40] *Igros Moshe Even HaEzer* 1:102.

Distractions

A couple should not have relations if they are distracted by something.[41] While having relations, a couple should not talk about anyone else or any mundane matter.[42] All thoughts, feelings and love should be directed to one's spouse or to *Hashem*. In the words of the *Igeres HaKodesh*,[43] "They should be thinking about the *mitzvos* they are doing, the possibility of creating holy souls, and that their attachment connects to holy sources and draws down the holy upper light."

Washing Hands

Ritually washing the hands before relations is recommended as a way of creating a spiritual mindset[44] and is compared to washing the hands before prayer.[45] It is a way of setting off this holy act from the realm of the mundane. This washing does not have to be done immediately before relations.[46]

Regarding washing one's hands ritually after relations, a couple should consult their *halachic* authority.[47]

Clothing and Covering

According to *Kabbalistic* and *halachic* sources, neither partner should be clothed at all during the act of relations,[48] as it is written, "A man should ... cleave to his wife, and they should become one flesh."[49]

---

[41] *Orach Chayim* 240:7.

[42] Ibid.

[43] *Igeres HaKodesh*, Ch. 5.

[44] *Mishnah Berurah* 240:54; *Yesod VeShoresh HaAvodah* 8:6; *Piskei Teshuvos* pg. 1015 ftn. 168.

[45] *Yesod VeShoresh HaAvodah* 8:6.

[46] As heard from Rav Yitzchak Berkovits.

[47] *Orach Chayim* 4:18 (citing *Mahari Abohav*, Ch. 7 quoting *Orchos Chayim*); *Yesod ViShoresh HaAvodah* 8:6; *Mishnah Berurah* 240:54 implies that one should wash one's hands immediately afterwards. This applies only if one is getting up, but not if one is going immediately to sleep (as heard by Rav Yitzchak Berkovits).

[48] *Kaf HaChayim* 240:60 quotes *Tikunei Zohar* 28; *Reishis Chachmah Shaar HaKedushah*, Ch. 16 quoting the *Zohar*. See also, *Sidur Beis Yaakov* (of Rab Yaakov Emden), *Hanhagas Leil Shabbos*, 7:2:6; *Gemara Kesubos* 48a. The *Shulchan Aruch* (*Even HaEzer* 76:13) rules that insisting on being clothed during relations is sufficient grounds for divorce. Rashi (*Shabbos* 13a) understands that this is the way a couple usually has relations. *Shaar HaTziyun* 240:18 quotes *Yad Aharon* quoting *kabbalistic* sources that it is preferred if they wear no clothes at all.

[49] *Bereishis* 2:24.

During the act of relations, a couple should be under some kind of cover, for example, a blanket or a sheet.[50]

Timing

A husband is obligated to have relations with his wife on the night that she goes to the *mikveh* and, if the wife is not *niddah*, on the night before he leaves on a trip,[51] if the wife desires (as with every time[52]). In addition, it is a *mitzvah* for a couple to have relations on Friday night.[53]

The couple may have relations as often as they are truly expressing love for one another. However, having marital relations should never be relegated to a mere physical act nor be done out of habit.[54]

Practices

Relations should be consummated while each partner is facing the other, with the husband above his wife.[55] A husband is allowed to see any part of his wife's body, except the vaginal area;[56] and he is permitted to kiss her anywhere except for the vaginal area.[57] A wife is allowed to see, touch or kiss any part of her husband that they desire, provided it does not cause spilling of seed.[58]

---

[50] *Tosafos* (*Niddah* 17a s.v. *Umashtin*) quotes a version of the *Gemara* that states, "God hates someone who has relations while naked," which is understood by *Mor U'Ketziyah* (to 240), *Mishnah Berurah* 240:36 and by *Peirush Maharzu* (to *Midrash Rabbah* to *Vayikra* 21:8) to mean without a cover on top of them.

[51] *Orach Chayim* 240:1.

[52] Ibid.

[53] *Orach Chayim* 280:1. See also *Sidur Beis Yaakov, Hanhagas Leil Shabbos*, where Rav Yaakov Emden describes his instructions on intimacy as "the *halachos* of *Shabbos* night."

[54] As heard from Rav Yitzchak Berkovits, Rama, *Even HaEzer* 25:2 states, "A man is permitted to have relations with his wife whenever he wants." It is understood here that she is not *niddah* and the relations take place with her consent.

[55] *Orach Chayim* 240:5. *Sefer Chassidim* 509 recommends that relations be consummated face-to-face.

[56] *Nedarim* 20a; *Orach Chayim* 240:4.

[57] *Orach Chayim* 240:4 and Rama, *Even HaEzer* 25:2. Couples with specific circumstances should consult their *halachic* authority.

[58] See Rama, *Even HaEzer* 25:2.

Spilling seed

If a husband and wife are in the process leading to relations and the husband cannot control himself and releases semen outside his wife's body, he is considered to have wasted seed.[59] This prohibition is derived from the *Torah*, which relates the story of Onan who intentionally spilled his seed in order not to impregnate Tamar.[60]

However, a husband is permitted — indeed, even obligated to — have relations with his wife even at a time when she cannot conceive. In this case, none of the seed is considered wasted, since once it enters the woman's body, it affects spiritual realms.[61]

Location

A couple should not have relations outdoors, even in a place where no one can see them. Nor should they have relations while lying on the ground. This is so that they do not imitate the ways of the animal kingdom.[62]

A couple should not have relations when others can hear them.[63] In addition, if they are guests in someone else's home, a couple should use their own sheets or towel underneath them for reasons of modesty.[64]

A couple may have relations while children (who are old enough to talk) are in the room if they are asleep.[65] An infant who is not yet talking may be awake but must be in a separate bed.[66]

A couple should not have relations or be completely unclothed in front of uncovered books containing *Torah* (in Hebrew or any language).[67] Any book or

---

[59] *Mishnah Berurah* quotes in 240:36; Rambam, *Hilchos Issurei Bi'ah* 21:9.
[60] *Bereishis* 38.
[61] *Mishnah Berurah* 240:2.
[62] Rambam, *Hilchos Issurei Bi'ah* 21:14; *Even HaEzer* 25:4.
[63] *Orach Chayim* 240:7.
[64] *Orach Chayim* 240:13; *Beis Shmuel* 25:7.
[65] *Orach Chayim* 240:6.
[66] *Orach Chayim* 240:16.
[67] *Orach Chayim* 240:6 and 40:2 with Rama.

even piece of paper containing three words or more of *Torah* should either be placed outside the bedroom or have a double cover over it.[68]

This *halachah* may seem puzzling, since we have discussed that when a husband and wife have marital relations in the proper way, the relations are a holy act. However, since the sin in the Garden of Eden, the possibility always exists that the act of relations can contain unholy elements.[69]

Special Considerations — The Nine Middos

The *Gemara* mentions nine *middos*, characteristics or states of mind or body, that can affect the soul of an unborn child.[70] A couple who has relations in any one of the following states risks damaging themselves or having children that will be spiritually blemished, potentially sinful and rebellious:[71]

1. *Forced* — meaning that the woman is not interested at the time in being intimate;

2. *Hated* — meaning that the husband despises his wife at the time yet wants to derive physical pleasure from her;

3. *Excommunicated* — some include in this category a mourner during the seven days of *shivah* ;[72]

---

[68] A double cover means that the item is covered with two coverings, one of which is not specific for *kedushah*, holiness. For example, in order to "double cover" *tefilin*, a cover could be placed on top of the *tefilin* bag. The first cover, the *tefilin* bag, is specific to the *tefilin*, the second cover is not. (If the *tefilin* bag itself is kept in a plastic bag made for this purpose, then both bags are considered specific to the *tefilin*.)

[69] As heard from Rav Yitzchak Berkovits.

[70] *Nedarim* 20b; see also *Orach Chayim* 140:3.

[71] Regarding damage to either or both of them, see Raavad in *Shaar HaKedushah*, quoted by *Beis Yosef* to 240. The concept of a "blemished soul" means that it has a lot of *yetzer harah* (evil inclinations) and bad character traits that will require much work to repair. However, it is not predestined to be evil. Thus, correction of its *middos* (character traits) will be harder but very doable (see *Kehilos Yaakov, Yevamos* 49 and *Igros Moshe Even HaEzer* 4:14). Studying *Torah* is mentioned as a method of *tikun* (correction).

[72] Tur to 240, quoting Raavad; *Bi'ur Halachah* to 240:3.

4. When the man believes he is having relations with a different woman;[73]
5. When she does not want to remain married to him but the physical relationship is not forced;
6. When drunk;[74]
7. When he has decided to divorce her;
8. When he fantasizes about a different woman;
9. If she verbally requested relations in a direct manner.

Nursing a Baby

According to *Kabbalah*,[75] a woman should not nurse a baby immediately after having relations for a minimum of 18 minutes.[76] However, Rav Yaakov Emden says, "If the baby is crying, and she cannot quiet him without nursing him, she should nurse him without being concerned."[77]

---

[73] This is akin to adultery.

[74] *Mishnah Berurah* 240:18 explains that this refers to drinking enough to be disoriented, but does not include having just a small amount of alcohol.

[75] *Zohar* quoted by *Beis Yosef* in *Bedek HaBayis* (end of 240) and *Magen Avraham* 240:29; see also *Sidur Beis Yaakov* (of Rav Yaakov Emden), *Hanhagas Leil Shabbos* 7:3:12.

[76] The amount of time quoted is the time is takes to walk 1-2 *mil*. A mil is a measure of distance 2000 amos (approximately one kilometer) but is used extensively by our Sages to measure time, as in the amount of time it takes to walk a mil. There is a three-way dispute among the *rishonim* whether the "time it takes to walk a *mil*" means 18 minutes, 22 1/2 minutes, or 24 minutes.

[77] *Sidur Beis Yaakov* (of Rav Yaakov Emden), *Hanhagas Leil Shabbos* 7:3:12.

CHAPTER 10

♦

Anticipating Your Period

When you are anticipating your period, *veses*, there are certain times that Jewish law requires a partial separation from your husband.[1] The *mitzvah* of calculating these times — and abstaining from marital relations during them — are so that the wife doesn't become *niddah* during relations.[2]

Sometimes a woman's period comes quite regularly; at other times her cycle can be quite irregular. Our Sages took into account both of these possibilities when formulating these separation times. They gave us a way to anticipate the onset of *niddah*, while living our lives and serving *Hashem* in a relaxed and confident manner. Adhering to their guidelines, in addition to paying attention to the nuances of one's own body, will assure that the transition to being *niddah* will not be stressful to you or your husband.

How the Separation Times Work: A Basic Outline

The segments of times that you will determine to be your "separate times"

---

[1] See *Yoreh Deah* 189 and commentaries.

[2] See Ch. 3 for a discussion of the consequence of *kares* incurred for marital relations while *niddah*. Regarding the separation times (*onos*), there is a dispute among the *halachic* authorities as to whether these separation times are rabbinically prohibited or prohibited by *Torah* (see Rama, *Yoreh Deah* 184:10; *Shach* 184:5; *Shu't Chasam Sofer Yoreh Deah* 170, 179; *Aruch HaShulchan* 184:4,5).

depend on whether you have a *halachically* regular period or a *halachically* irregular period. Below you will find a definition of each of these types of periods.

These segments of time are called *onos* (or, in the singular, *onah*). Each Jewish day is divided into two *onos*: The nighttime *onah*, which lasts from sunset to sunrise; and the daytime *onah*, which lasts from sunrise to sunset.[3]

In general, your separation times will be determined by the segment of the day, or *onah*, when your last period began. For example, if your last period began in the afternoon, you will calculate your required separation times for the next month based on the daytime *onah*, that is, from sunrise to sunset.[4] If your last period began at night, you will calculate your separation times based on the nighttime *onah*, from sunset to sunrise. We will discuss below, in detail, how to make these calculations.

During these separation *onos*, marital relations are forbidden.[5] Hugging and kissing are allowed;[6] but not recommended.[7] Some also refrain from sleeping in the same bed.[8] It is a good idea to let your husband know a number of days in advance the dates and times of your separation *onos*.

The *harchakos* that we discussed in Chapter 4, such as passing objects to one another, serving food directly to each other and the like, do not apply during the separation *onos*.[9]

During these separation times, *bedikos* are made to check if indeed your period

---

3   *Chavos Daas* 184:5. This is accepted as normative *halachah*, although *Aruch HaShulchan* 184:27 rules that the delineation between day and night for separation *onos* is determined by daybreak (*alos hashachar*) and nightfall (*tzeis hakochavim*).

4   *Yoreh Deah* 184:2 and *Chavos Daas* 184:5.

5   *Yoreh Deah* 184:2.

6   Ibid.

7   Especially if it is passionate.

8   *Taz* 184:3 prohibits, whereas *Bach* 184 and *Shach* recommend refraining. *Taharas Yisrael* (184 ftn 21) and *Shiurei Shevet HaLevi* (on *Shach* 184:6) say that although hugging and kissing is only prohibited as a *chumrah* (stringency), if it leads to *hotzaas zera levatalah* (wasting seed), then it is prohibited. *Shiurei Shevet HaLevi* also mentions that if a couple was stringent on hugging and kissing (and knew that it was not required) and now want to stop being *machmir*, that they should do *hataras nedarim*, annulling of vows.

9   *Yoreh Deah* 184:2.

has arrived. The first *bedikah* is made at the beginning of the *onah*, and another is made towards the end of the *onah*.[10] If your *onah* falls out in the nighttime, make a *bedikah* before you go to sleep. It is preferable to make an additional *bedikah* when you wake up.[11]

If making *bedikos* is difficult, only one *bedikah* is required,[12] preferably towards the end of the *onah*. If you are concerned that making *bedikos* can irritate an existing condition (for example, a wound, infection or any other type of vaginal condition that bleeds easily), consult your *halachic* authority.

If one of your separation times coincides either with a night right before your husband is scheduled to leave on a trip or the night you are scheduled to go to the *mikveh*, consult your *halachic* authority.[13]

How to Calculate Your Separation Times: An Overview

Your monthly separation times will depend on whether you have a *halachically* regular period, *veses kavua*, or a *halachically* irregular period, *veses she'ayna kavua*.

In the following sections, you will find the definitions of both types of periods and their required separation times. Even if you don't have a regular period, it is

---

[10] *Badei HaShulchan* 184:54.

[11] *Shiurei Shevet HaLevi* 184:9:4.

[12] *Taharas Yisrael* 184:66 ftn 144; *Yoreh Deah* 184:9 also implies that only one *bedikah* is necessary.

[13] The *Shulchan Aruch* (*Yoreh Deah* 184:10) rules that if the husband is leaving on a trip, the couple may have relations even though it is a separation *onah*. Rama (ibid.) rules that it is permitted for them to have relations, but it is preferable if the husband spends time with his wife and gives her attention without having relations. *Shu't Chasam Sofer*, quoted by *Pischei Teshuvah* ad loc. 184:22, forbids relations in this circumstance. In the context of these comments of the *Shulchan Aruch* and Rama, the *poskim* discuss what is the *halachah* if her separation *onah* falls out on a *mikveh* night. Some authorities rule that she should go to the *mikveh*, and that they may have relations (*Keneses Yechezkel*, *Gilyon* Maharsha, and *Atzei Levonah*, all quoted by *Shiurei Shevet HaLevi* 184:2). However, most rule that they may not have relations. The question then arises as to whether or not the wife should go to the *mikveh* that night, since they are allowed to hug and kiss. Again, there is a dispute among the *poskim*. For further discussion, see *Pischei Teshuvah* 184:22 and *Shiurei Shevet HaLevi* 184:2.

helpful to be familiar with the different types of regular patterns, as many of the same principles will be applied to an irregular period. In addition, you will then be aware of what patterns fulfill the requirements of a *veses kavua* in case you notice similar patterns in your own cycle.

Because calculating these separation times can be complicated, it is highly recommended that you or your husband consult with your *halachic* authority a few months after you are married, and every six months or so thereafter for the first two years of your marriage to make sure the calculations are correct.

The following are the main principles of these laws, of which an understanding is crucial to be able to calculate your separation *onos* correctly. Although making these calculations may sound complex at first, after you are accustomed to doing so, it will much easier.

- ♦ Your calculations will be based on when your last period or periods arrived.

- ♦ When calculating your separation times, most *halachic* authorities rule that the count only begins from an actual flow of blood, not from any pre-period staining (even if the staining has already made you *niddah*).[14] Some rule otherwise. If your period is preceded by staining or spotting, ask your *halachic* authority from which day you should begin your count.

- ♦ Similarly, if you normally experience spotting or staining (even if it does not render you *niddah*), ask your *halachic*

---

[14] *Yoreh Deah* 190:54 rules that a stain discovered on a *bedikah* cloth is counted for *vesasos* but not other stains. This is the prevalent practice in America. However, Rav Wosner (from Israel) in *Shiurei Shevet HaLevi* states that the accepted practice is not to count *veses* from a *bedikah* but only a flow. Rav Moshe Feinstein rules that if a woman stains before her period flow starts, she should count from the staining if one of the following two situations exist: (1) If she usually does not sense when her period starts, or (2) if, three times in a row, she stained a *kesem* that made her *tamei* before her period started (even if she usually senses when her period starts). However, if there is a day's interruption where there was neither staining nor flow, Rav Moshe rules that one counts the *veses* from the flow, not from the previous staining.

authority if this is an indicator of a *halachically* regular period.[15]

◆ If you are uncertain on which *onah* your period began, the later *onah* is counted as the time your period began.[16] For example, if you notice that your period has already begun when you awaken in the morning (and you are unsure as to whether it began in the night or after sunrise, your period is considered to have begun during the daytime *onah*.

◆ If your period begins close to the beginning of the morning or close to the end of the afternoon, note the time and compare it with the time of sunrise or sunset to make sure you are counting from the correct *onah*.

◆ When making your calculations for your separation times, the amount of days your period lasts is not important.[17] What is important to your calculations is the day the flow began. (See ftn.)

◆ In all the *halachos* of *vesasos* (and thus in all the calculations of the separation times), we only use the Hebrew calendar.[18]

A Veses Kavua: A Regular Period

The establishment of a *veses kavua* depends on seeing the same pattern three times in a row.[19] Some regular periods have patterns that are easily recognizable;

---

[15] This situation may also be considered a regular *veses haguf.* See *Igros Moshe* 3:51.

[16] *Yoreh Deah* 184:4. However, *Badei HaShulchan* 184:31, quoting many early *poskim,* rules that both *onos* are counted as the *veses.*

[17] *Yoreh Deah* 184:6, with the exception of Lubavitcher *chassidim* and others who follow the *Shulchan Aruch HaRav,* where the interval is calculated from the end of the previous period to the beginning of the next one.

[18] *Shu't Minchas Yitzchak* 6:54:3.

[19] *Yoreh Deah* 189:2.

others may not, even though they may *halachically* fall under this category. If your period does not fall into one of the patterns that are discussed below, but nevertheless has a pattern, be sure to consult your *halachic* authority.

Common Types of Regular Periods

A Period Determined by the Date: Veses HaChodesh

The most obvious type of period determined by the date is called a *Veses HaChodesh* (*chodesh* means month in Hebrew). This is a period that follows a pattern based on the same day of the Hebrew month. If your period begins on the same *onah* every third of the Hebrew month three times in a row (for example, during the daytime of the third of *Nisan*, the third of *Iyar* and the third of *Sivan*), you have established a regular period based on the date.

An unusual *veses kavua* determined by the date could be a cycle that has a pattern of a consistent increase (or decrease) of days every month. If you notice such a pattern, consult your *halachic* authority.

A Period Determined by Interval: Veses HaFlagah

A *veses* that arrives after the same number of days every month — and during the same *onah* — is called a *veses haflagah kavua*, a regular period determined by intervals.[20] The interval is determined by counting as follows: Day One is the day your second-to-the-last period began. The last day of the count is the day your last period began.[21] Note that the amount of days your period lasts does not affect the count when determining the number of days in your interval.[22] What is im-

---

[20] *Yoreh Deah* 189:1—2, 13.
[21] *Yoreh Deah* 189:2
[22] With the exception of Lubavitcher *chassidim* and any others who follow the *Shulchan Aruch HaRav*, where the interval is calculated from the end of the previous period to the beginning of the next one.

portant to your calculations is the day the flow began. (See exception in ftn. 22 above.)

As with the establishment of every *halachically* regular period, this pattern must be seen three cycles in a row. Thus, to establish this pattern, it will take four periods (which, in turn, make three intervals).

A Period Determined by Physical Symptom: Veses HaGuf

A *veses kavua* can also be established by experiencing (three times in a row) some specific physical symptom that precedes the onset of a period.[23] For example, if your period is preceded by staining, even if the color and size do not make you *niddah*, you may be able to establish a *veses haguf kavua* (*guf* means body in Hebrew).

More commonly, if the onset of your period is frequently preceded by abdominal cramping or swelling, this may also be a sign of a regular *veses haguf*.[24] If you notice that any specific, especially unusual, physical sensation that regularly accompanies the onset of your period arrives, consult your *halachic* authority.

Other Types of Regular Periods

The above examples are the most common of the *halachically* regular periods. Less common patterns include a cycle based on weeks, called a *veses hashavua*. In this pattern, you would see that your period consistently arrives on the same day of the week — and during the same *onah* — for example, every fourth Monday in the morning.[25]

---

23 *Yoreh Deah* 189:19. The *Gemara* and *poskim* mention, for example, excessive yawning and abdominal cramping. A *veses haguf* can also be *ayna kavua* (irregular), which means that if one time a woman had an unusual symptom that preceded the onset of her period, then the next time this symptom happens, she needs to be concerned about the onset of her period. (See section below on *veses haguf* for irregular periods.)

24 *Yoreh Deah* 189:19, based on *Niddah* 63a.

25 To establish a *veses haflagah kavua*, four periods are required since the interval must be repeated three times to create a permanent pattern. A *veses hashavua* requires only three

A regular period can also be established by a combination of factors. For example, the above *veses hashavua* might be combined with a physical sensation. Thus, a woman might find that her period consistently arrives every fourth Sunday, but only when preceded by a specific sensation.

Similarly, a woman might find that her period only arrives every other month but on the same day of the Hebrew month. She could also find that her period arrives in an unusual but consistent pattern (either by intervals or dates) — for example, after 24, 26, 29, 24, 26, 29, 24, 26, 29 days.

Halachically regular patterns can be quite complicated to determine. Moreover, you might not even notice that your period has such a pattern. This is one of the reasons why it is a good idea to keep a written record of the time and date your period arrives, noting any specific physical sensation that accompanies its onset. After a few months, review your records. If you notice any patterns, consult your *halachic* authority. Recording your period on a calendar where you can see an entire year at one time can help identify a possible long-term pattern.

If your period is not regular, but consistently arrives after more than thirty days, see the section below *A Period That Always Arrives After Thirty Days*. If your period is regulated by hormones, see also the relevant section below.

---

periods, since it is the repeating day of the week that creates the *veses*, not the interval. Thus, a *veses hashavua* that is *kavua* will be established one period earlier than a *veses haflagah kavua* (*Toras HaShelamim* 189:9). However, if a woman creates a *veses hashavua* and then sees her period on her anticipated day the next month, does she have a *veses hashavua* or a *veses haflagah* or both? *Chavos Daas* 189:4 rules that she has only a *veses haflagah* (because the *haflagah* is the more likely cause for her period than the day of the week; thus the preexisting *veses hashavua* is preempted by the new *veses haflagah*). This can make a difference on a practical matter if, in a future month, she misses her day of the week/*haflagah* date, but her period begins on it two months later. When is her separation *onah* now? If her *veses* is established by seeing her period every fourth Monday, for example, it is still on Monday. If her *veses* is established by seeing every 29th day, then it is 29 days from her last period, regardless of the day of the week. The result of this ruling is that as a practical matter, a woman who has a *veses hashavua* usually has such a *veses* for only a short period of time; either it becomes a *haflagah* or it ends. (It could last for a while in the unlikely case where she misses that day of week the next month, thus avoiding creating a *haflagah*, and then sees on that day of week one of the next two months, thus keeping her *veses hashavua* active.)

When to Separate for a Regular Period

The required separation time for a *veses kavua* (with the exception of a *veses haguf kavua*) is the *onah* in which you are expecting your period. For example, if you have established a pattern where your period always arrives every 28 days during the night, you are required to separate on the 28th day after your last period arrived, from sunset to sunrise. For a *veses haguf kavua*, the separation *onah* is required whenever the physical symptom occurs.

For those who follow the stringency of the *Ohr Zarua* (see the section below for further discussion), the separation time begins the *onah* before you expect your period to arrive.

Requirements of the Separation Time for a Regular Period

As we discussed above, during these separation times, *bedikos* are made to check if indeed your period has arrived. The first *bedikah* is made at the beginning of the *onah* and another is made towards the end of the *onah*.[26] If your *onah* falls out in the nighttime, make a *bedikah* before you go to sleep and, preferably, an additional one when you wake up.[27]

If the *bedikah* is free from any *niddah* color, you may resume a full physical relationship with your husband when the *onah* ends.[28] In addition, you should verbally tell your husband that you have made a *bedikah*.[29]

If making *bedikos* is difficult, only one *bedikah* is required,[30] preferably towards the end of the *onah*. If you forgot to make a *bedikah* during the *onah*, you are re-

---

[26] *Badei HaShulchan* 184:54.
[27] *Shiurei Shevet HaLevi* 184:9:4.
[28] Even though your *halachic* requirement of separation is over, it is advisable to pay attention to any indications that your period might begin during subsequent days.
[29] *Yoreh Deah* 184:11.
[30] *Taharas Yisrael* 184:66 ftn 144.

quired to make a *bedikah* before resuming relations with your husband, even if your period has not appeared.[31]

When a Regular Period Turns Irregular

Just as it takes three consecutive periods to establish a *veses kavua*, it also takes three consecutive periods to "deactivate" a pattern.[32] For example, if your period arrived three cycles in a row at a time different from your regular *veses*, your *veses kavua* is deactivated. However, some authorities contend that, even in these circumstances, a *veses kavua* can only be deactivated if the required *bedikos* were made during each separation *onah* and they were free from any *niddah* color. If the *bedikos* were not made, the *veses kavua* is not deactivated.[33] Others disagree.[34]

Once your *veses kavua* is deactivated, you now have the status of a woman with a *halachically* irregular period and are obligated to keep the separation *onos* required for this type of period.

However, if your period reverts back to its old pattern — even once — your *veses kavua* is reactivated.[35] In fact, your *veses kavua* — whether active or not — is never totally cancelled, unless you establish a new *veses kavua*.[36]

What happens if one time — or even two consecutive times — your period comes at a time other than on your regular *onah*? You still have an active *veses kavua*.[37] However, these variances will affect when you are required to separate from your husband the next month when anticipating your period.

---

[31]   *Yoreh Deah* 189:4. This *halachah* only applies for a *veses kavua*.

[32]   *Yoreh Deah* 189:2, 14–15.

[33]   Ramban, *Hilchos Niddah* 5:19. This is different from a *veses she'ayna kavua*, which is wiped out even if the *bedikah* was forgotten. See also *Chavos Daas* 184:10.

[34]   Some authorities contend that even a *veses kavua* can be eliminated if she forgot to make a *bedikah* provided she paid attention and/or was wearing tight fitting undergarments (see *Shu't Cheishev Ha'Eifod* 1:126).

[35]   *Yoreh Deah* 189:15.

[36]   *Yoreh Deah* 189:15.

[37]   *Yoreh Deah* 189:14.

Specifically, if your period arrives once or twice at a time other than your regular *onah*, the next month you are required to separate on three *onos*:

- Your regular *onah* of your *veses kavua*,

- The *haflagah* (the interval — see below for how to calculate this *onah*) of the irregular period, and

- The *yom hachodesh* (the same day of the Hebrew month — see below for how to calculate this *onah*) of the irregular period.

A Veses She'Ayna Kavua: An Irregular Period

Most women today find that they do not have a regular period as defined by *halachah*. Our Sages have also given these women a way to anticipate their periods by identifying certain times during the month when a woman's period is likely to arrive.[38]

For women with irregular periods, these times will be your separation *onos* in anticipation of your next cycle.

When to Separate for an Irregular Period

Women with irregular periods are required to separate on the following *onos*:

1. The Yom HaChodesh: The Same Day of the Hebrew Month

This is the same day of the Hebrew month on which your last period arrived. For example, if you got your period on the 20th of *Tammuz* during the daytime, you are required to separate the next month on the 20th of Av during the daytime *onah* (from sunrise to sunset).[39] To calculate this *onah*, only the Hebrew calendar is used. (For those who keep the *Ohr Zarua onah*, see below for more information.)

---

[38] See *Yoreh Deah* 189: 2, 4, 13.

[39] In addition, if your current cyle is significantly shorter than your pervious cycle (for example,

If your previous period arrived on a later date than your current period, but you were still bleeding on the date of the previous period, there is a dispute as to whether or not you are required to separate on the earlier *onah* as well.[40] For example, let's say that your second to the last period arrived on the 7th of *Nissan* and your last period arrived on the 5th of *Iyar*. On the 7th of *Iyar*, you were still bleeding (as it was the third day of your period). According to most *halachic* authorities, you will now have two *onos* for the *yom hachodesh* the following month: The 5th of *Sivan* and the 7th of *Sivan*.[41] Other authorities rule that in this situation, there is no carry over of the *yom hachodesh onah* from the previous month since this month the bleeding transpired in the middle of your period.[42] Ask your *halachic* authority which opinion to follow.

♦ If your period arrived on the 30th of the month (the first day of a two-day *Rosh Chodesh*) and the next month only has 29 days, most *halachic* authorities say the next month's *yom hachodesh* is observed on the first of the next month.[43]

2. The HaFlagah: The Interval Day

This is the number of days that intervened between your last two periods. If, for example, there were 28 days between your last two periods, you are required to separate on the 28th day after your last period.[44]

The *haflagah*, or interval, is calculated as follows: Count as Day One the day

---

your period arrived two weeks early), then you will also need to separate on your previous *yom hachodesh onah* as well, even if this might occur shorly after your *mikveh* night. For example, if your second to the last period arrived on the first of the month of *Nissan*, and your last period arrived two weeks later on the 15th of *Nissan*, you must separate the following month on both the first of *Iyar* and the 15th of *Iyar*. Rama, *Yoreh Deah* 189:13.

[40] Note that all *halachic* authorities agree that if the *yom hachodesh* passes and she does not see blood on that day, the *veses* is uprooted.

[41] *Shulchan Aruch HaRav* 189:38, 68; *Igros Moshe Yoreh Deah* 1:122; *Shu't Minchas Yitzchak* 8:74; *Shiurei Shevet HaLevi* 189:13:14.

[42] *Posayach Shaar*, pg. 252.

[43] *Aruch HaShulchan* 189:12; *Shiurei Shevet HaLevi* 189:6:4.

[44] *Yoreh Deah* 189:2.

your second to the last period began. End your count the day your last period began.[45] You now have the number of days that intervened between your last two periods. Now begin counting again to calculate your separation day for the next cycle. This time, begin the count from the day your last period began. As we discussed above, the amount of days your period lasts does not affect the count when determining the number of days in your interval.[46] (For exceptions, see the ftn. 45.)

The *onah* on which you and your husband separate depends on the time of day when your last period arrived. For example, if your last period arrived during the nighttime, then your *haflagah* separation *onah* will take place from sunset to sunrise.

(For those who keep the *Ohr Zarua onah*, see below for more information.)

- In addition, some *halachic* authorities rule that if your previous interval was greater than your current interval, you also need to separate on this *onah* as well.[47] For example, if your current interval was 28 days and your previous interval was 29 days, you would have two *haflagah* intervals the next month, the 28th and the 29th day. Other authorities rule that there is no carry over of the *haflagah onah* from the previous month.[48] Ask a question to your *halachic* authority as to which opinion to follow.

3. The Beinonis: The Thirtieth Day

The *beinonis* (average or median) is the thirtieth day from the day your last period arrived.[49] An easy way to calculate the *onah beinonis* is that it will be four weeks plus one (Hebrew) calendar day after your last period arrived.[50] As with

---

45 *Yoreh Deah* 190:54, with the exception of those who follow the *Shulchan Aruch HaRav*.
46 Ibid.
47 *Beis Meir* to 189:13.
48 *Shach* in *Nekudos HaKesef* on *Taz* 189:18.
49 *Yoreh Deah* 189:1.
50 *Sidrei Taharah* 189, end of 31. This is the most widely held opinion on how to calculate the

the above separation times, the *onah* on which you are required to separate depends on the *onah* in which your period arrived the previous month.[51]

4. Veses HaGuf: Physical Symptom

Anytime an unusual physical symptom — for example, excessive yawning,
cramping, swelling[52] — precedes the onset of your period, you need to be concerned that it will happen again. If you do notice the same symptom again, you
must separate on that *onah*.[53] This is called an irregular *veses haguf*. If this unusual
symptom precedes the onset of your period three times in a row, you have established a *veses haguf kavua*.

Requirements During the Separation Times
for an Irregular Period

During these separation times, *bedikos* are made to check if, indeed, your period has arrived. The first *bedikah* is made at the beginning of the *onah* and another
is made towards the end of the *onah*.[54] If your *onah* falls out in the nighttime, make
one *bedikah* before you go to sleep and preferably another one when you wake
up.[55]

If the *bedikah* is free from any *niddah* color, you may resume a full physical rela-

---

onah beinonis. A minority of *halachic* authorities rule that the *onah beinonis* is the 31st day. (See *Chavos Daas* 189:12, who rules that the count of *onah beinonis* does not include the day of the previous period, i.e., it is 30 days after the previous period, not including the day of the previous period. For simplicity sake, this is usually referred to as the "31st day.")

51 Some rule like Pleisi 189:15 who contends that the separation lasts the entire Jewish day from sunset to sunset. Pleisi is of the opinion that the *onah beinonis* has nothing to do with which *onah* the previous period arrived on. His logical basis is that this is not a repeating period, but a generic estimate that a woman usually gets her period about 30 days after her previous period.

52 *Yoreh Deah* 189:19, based on *Niddah* 63a.

53 *Yoreh Deah* 189:26.

54 *Badei HaShulchan* 184:54.

55 *Shiurei Shevet HaLevi* 184:9:4.

tionship with your husband after the *onah* ends.[56] If making *bedikos* is difficult, only one *bedikah* is required,[57] preferably towards the end of the *onah*.

If you forgot to make any *bedikos*, and the separation time is already over (with no indication that your period has arrived), you are not obligated to make a *bedikah*, with the exception of the *onah beinonis*.[58]

A Period That Always Arrives After Thirty Days

There is a dispute among *halachic* authorities as to whether a woman whose period usually comes after more than 30 days needs to separate on the *yom hachodesh* and *onah beinonis*. If you find that your period regularly comes after 30 days, check with your *halachic* authority as to which opinion to follow.[59]

A Period Determined by Hormonal Pills

Many *halachic* authorities rule that a period regulated (or caused) by hormone medications has different rules in terms of *onos*. Check with your *halachic* authority as to when you need to separate if your period is regulated by synthetic hormones.[60]

The Ohr Zarua Onah

Some *halachic* authorities rule that in addition to the required *onos* discussed above (for either *halachically* regular or *halachically* irregular periods), a couple

---

[56] Even though your *halachic* requirements of separation are over, it is advisable to pay attention to any indications that your period might begin during subsequent days.

[57] *Taharas Yisrael* 184:66 ftn. 144.

[58] *Yoreh Deah* 184:11.

[59] See *Shu't Shoel U'Meishiv* 3:2:46; *Sidrei Taharah* 189:20; *Chavos Daas* 186:3; *Taharas Yisrael* 186:13; *Igros Moshe Yoreh Deah* 2:72.

[60] *Nishmas Avraham* 2 pg. 95 quoting Rav Shlomo Zalman Auerbach; *Shu't Minchas Yitzchak* 1:127; *Shu't Shevet HaLevi* 4:99:9; *Shiurei Shevet HaLevi* 184:8:2 & 189:23:5; *Shu't Tzitz Eliezer* 13:103; *Marei Kohen* pg. 152; 184.

should separate as well for the twelve-hour period that falls before each *onah*.[61] Thus, if your required separation *onah* falls during the daytime (from sunrise to sunset), the separation would begin the previous night at sunset.

This approach follows the opinion of the *Ohr Zarua*. Many authorities maintain this additional separation is not required.[62] Check with your *halachic* authority as to which opinion to follow.[63] If a woman's night to go to the *mikveh* coincides with an *Ohr Zarua onah*, she is allowed to go to the *mikveh* and have marital relations.[64]

Setting Up a Calendar for an Irregular Period: A Step-by-Step Guide

Make sure you have a Jewish calendar that is easy for you to read and has enough space on each date to record the following information:

Step One: When your period arrives, make a note on the appropriate day of your calendar. Record the *onah* in which it arrived, as well as any specific physical sensations (or staining) that preceded its onset. Some women find it helpful to choose a symbol — for example, a check mark — which they use consistently on their calendars to note the arrival of their period.

Step Two: Record your next *yom hachodesh*, noting on your calendar the *onah* in which you are required to separate. For example, if your period began on the 20th of *Kislev* during the day, you will record the 20th of *Teves* (during the daytime *onah*) as your next *yom hachodesh*. (If you need to be concerned about any previous dates, as discussed above, make a note on your calendar of that *onah* as well.)

---

[61] Opinion of *Ohr Zarua*, end of Ch. 358; see also *Shach* 184:7 and *Nekudos HaKesef* ad loc.; *Shiurei Shevet HaLevi* 184:2, pg. 22.

[62] *Yoreh Deah* 184:2 and *Taz* ad loc. 2; *Chazon Ish* in appendix to *Taharas Bas Yisrael* 6. *Rama*, *Yoreh Deah* 184:10.

[63] For a further discussion on when it is appropriate to keep stringencies, see "The Weighing of Saintliness," Ch. 20 in the classic work, *Path of the Just* by Rav Moshe Chaim Luzzatto. For general attitude on stringencies, see *Michtav Mei'Eliyahu*, Vol. 3, pg. 294, by Rav Eliyahu Dessler.

[64] *Pischei Teshuvah* 184:22.

Some women find it helpful to use a consistent symbol on their calendars to note the separation *onos* — for example, an "x."

Step Three: Record your next *onah beinonis*, noting again the appropriate *onah* in which you are required to separate. This is the thirtieth day after the arrival of your period.[65]

Step Four: Record your next *haflagah onah*. This is the number of days that intervened between your last two periods. Count as *Day One* the day your second to the last period began. End your count the day your last period began. You now have the number of days that intervened between your last two periods. Now begin counting again to calculate your next *haflagah onah*. This time, begin the count from the day your last period began. (If you need to be concerned about any previous dates, as discussed above, make a note on your calendar of that *onah* as well.)

If you have just begun to keep a record of your periods, you will not have a *haflagah onah* until you have recorded two periods.

Pregnancy, After Childbirth and Menopause
— When do the Separation Times Apply?

The above three categories are times when a woman's cycle is not expected. Therefore, women in these categories have certain exemptions from the laws of *vesasos*. We will look at each category and discuss when you must observe various separation times.

Pregnancy

Onah Requirements for a Woman Who Has a Halachically Irregular Period: The Beginning of Pregnancy

Most women find out they are pregnant after they miss their first period. For

---

[65] With the exception of those who hold that the *onah beinonis* occurs on the 31st day and/or those who hold that the *onah beinonis* is a 24-hour separation, as discussed above.

the majority of women who have *halachically* irregular periods, this will mean that they will have observed their separation *onos* — the *yom hachodesh*, *haflagah* and *beinonis* — the first month of their pregnancy. Once these *onos* pass with no bleeding or period, they are henceforth uprooted, meaning one is no longer obligated to separate the next month.[66]

If you have a *halachically* irregular period and find out you are pregnant before your *onos* pass, most authorities rule that you are still obligated to keep these separation times the first month.[67]

Bleeding or Staining During Pregnancy for a Woman Who Has a Halachically Irregular Period: Onah Requirements

If a woman with a *halachically* irregular period bleeds and is rendered *niddah* during the first three months of pregnancy, the next month all the regular separation *onos* are observed.[68]

If a woman with a *halachically* irregular period bleeds and is rendered *niddah* after the first three months of pregnancy, the separation *onos* of the *yom hachodesh* and *haflagah* (if relevant) are observed the following month.[69] (There will only be a *haflagah* if she has bled two or more times after the third month of pregnancy.) There is no requirement to separate on the *beinonis*.[70]

---

[66] For a *halachically* irregular period, the *haflagah* and *beinonis* are measured only from the last period, which, in this case, was skipped. The *yom hachodesh* is cancelled after the first time the date arrived without a period.

[67] *Yoreh Deah* 184:7, 34. Rav Moshe Feinstein (*Igros Moshe Yoreh Deah* 3:52) disagrees and rules that the separation *onos* need not be observed if the pregnancy is medically confirmed. For a lengthy discussion of this topic, see Rav Eliyahu Falk, *Machazeh Eliyahu*, Ch. 105, and his sources there, including: *Midrash Rabbah* (*Parshas Tazria* 14:3), *Shu't Chasam Sofer Yoreh Deah* 169, *Shu't Avodas HaGershuni* 21, *Shu't Rabbi Akiva Eiger* 128; and *Shu't Avnei Nezer Yoreh Deah* 238:3.

[68] *Yoreh Deah* 189:34. For those who follow Rav Moshe Feinstein's opinion, only the *yom hachodesh* and *haflagah* would be required (*Yoreh Deah* 3:52).

[69] *Yoreh Deah* 189:33 and *Pischei Teshuvah* 189:31.

[70] *Shiurei Shevet HaLevi* 189:33:5; *Pischei Teshuvah* 189:31. However, *Shulchan Aruch HaRav* 189:114 rules that she must also keep the *onah beinonis*.

A *niddah*-colored stain (*kesem*) that renders a woman *niddah* does not usually count for *vesasos* (and hence, there are no separation *onos* based on this the following month). However, if a *niddah*-colored stain is found on a *bedikah* cloth, then the separation *onos* are usually required (in addition to all the laws of *niddah*). If you stain during pregnancy, check with your *halachic* authority if you are required to observe any *onos* the following month.[71]

Onah Requirements for a Woman
Who Has a Halachically Regular Period:
The Beginning of Pregnancy

For a woman who has an active *veses kavua* (*halachically* regular period), most authorities require that she observe her regular separation *onah* (or *onos*) for the first three months of the pregnancy.[72]

Bleeding or Staining During Pregnancy
for a Woman Who Has a Halachically Regular Period:
Onah Requirements

If a woman with a *halachically* regular period bleeds and is rendered *niddah* during the first three months of pregnancy, most *halachic* authorities rule that the normal *onos* are kept the following month.[73]

After the first three months, all *niddah* bleeding is treated by the same laws as those for a *halachically* irregular period during pregnancy, which means that if a

---

[71]   *Yoreh Deah* 190:54. The *Shulchan Aruch* rules that *vesasos* are required from blood on a *bedikah* cloth but not from a *kesem*. *Shiurei Shevet HaLevi* 190:54:7 writes that blood on a *bedikah* does not necessarily count towards a *veses*. *Igros Moshe Yoreh Deah* 3:51 rules that if a woman stains before her period (the flow) starts, she should count from the staining, but only if she usually does not sense when her period starts or if three times in a row she stained before her period started (even if she usually senses when her period starts). However, if there is a day's interruption when there was neither staining nor flow, Rav Moshe Feinstein rules that one counts the *veses* from the flow not the previous staining.

[72]   See ftn. 67.

[73]   *Yoreh Deah* 189:33, 44.

woman bleeds after the first three months of pregnancy, she is obligated to sepa-rate the next month on the *yom hachodesh* and the *haflagah* (if relevant) the follow-ing month.[74] (There will only be a *haflagah* if she has bled two or more times after the first three months of pregnancy.) There is no requirement to separate on the *beinonis*.[75]

Even if the bleeding occurs three times in a row in a pattern of a *halachically* regular period, a woman who is pregnant cannot establish a *veses kavua*.[76] Instead, the bleeding is treated as *veses she'ayna kavua*, which requires the *onos* of the *yom hachodesh* and *haflagah* (if relevant) to be observed the following month, but not the *beinonis*.[77]

A *niddah*-colored stain (*kesem*) that renders a woman *niddah* does not usually count for *vesasos* (and hence, there are no separation *onos* based on this the fol-lowing month). However, if a *niddah*-colored stain is found on a *bedikah* cloth, then the separation *onos* are usually required (in addition to all the laws of *niddah*). If you stain during pregnancy, check with your *halachic* authority if you are re-quired to observe any *onos* the following month.[78]

After Childbirth

The bleeding that accompanies childbirth and afterwards is not considered a period. Even though it is *niddah* blood (which requires the proper *taharah* proc-ess), no separation *onos* are calculated based on the onset of bleeding from child-birth.[79]

For the first 24 months after a woman gives birth, she has the status of a *meinekes*, a nursing mother (whether she is nursing her baby or not during this

---

[74] *Yoreh Deah* 189:33 and *Pischei Teshuvah* 189:31.

[75] *Shiurei Shevet HaLevi* 189:33:5.

[76] *Yoreh Deah* 189:33.

[77] *Yoreh Deah* 189:34, *Shiurei Shevet HaLevi* 189:33(5).

[78] *Yoreh Deah* 190:54. See ftn. 71 above.

[79] *Badei HaShulchan, Biurim* 189:33.

time).[80] The Sages in the *Gemara* ruled that a woman's period was unlikely to resume for these first 24 months since her body was recuperating from child-birth. Thus, since she needn't be concerned that her period would begin during this time, the *rishonim* rule that she was exempt from previously existing *vesasos*[81] and, moreover, cannot establish a *veses kavua* during the same time period.[82] A minority opinion in the *Gemara*[83] contends that the reason a woman's period didn't resume during this time was due to the child being nursed for these 24 months,[84] as was encouraged.[85]

In our day, since most women's periods resume much earlier than 24 months after giving birth (even when nursing), most contemporary *halachic* authorities rule that the laws of *vesasos* begin once a woman's period resumes.[86] For a woman who had a *veses she'ayna kavua* before her pregnancy, the calculations of her separation *onos* begin anew and are not carried over from before the pregnancy.[87]

A woman who had an active *veses kavua* before she become pregnant should consult her *halachic* authority if her period resumes within 24 months after giving birth to ascertain whether or not her *veses kavua* is active again or whether it is only considered active after 24 months.

Many women find that in the first weeks (even months) after birth, hormonal fluctuations as well as adjustments in a baby's nursing schedule can cause *niddah*

---

[80] *Niddah* 9a.

[81] The *rishonim* follow the Sages and rule that her concern for her *veses* is only after 24 months have transpired whether or not she is nursing (*Yoreh Deah* 189:7, 34).

[82] *Yoreh Deah* 189: 33. Even if she experienced three cycles in a row in a pattern of a *veses kavua*, each was treated as a *veses she'ayna kavua* since each period was considered an aberration.

[83] *Niddah* 9a.

[84] Thus, if a woman was not nursing, she should expect her period to resume.

[85] See *Pischei Teshuvah, Yoreh Deah* 81:16. *Kesubos* 39a and *Yevamos* 12b show us that it was normative at the time for a baby to be nursed for 18-24 months, and they imply that a significant amount of the baby's nutrition came from his mother during that time.

[86] *Igros Moshe Yoreh Deah* 3:52; *Marei Kohen* pg.161. See also *Shiurei Shevet HaLevi* 184:7(4). See also the discussion in *Tosafos Chadashim, Niddah* 1:4; *Shu't Chasam Sofer Yoreh Deah* 70 and *Lechem V'Simlah, Simlah* 189:54.

[87] Since they were uprooted by the pregnancy, according to the opinion of the majority of *poskim*. See *Shiurei Shevet HaLevi* 189:34.

bleeding. A woman in this situation should consult her *halachic* authority as to her requirements regarding *onos*.

Menopause

When a woman's period stops arriving, she will eventually have no separation *onos*, just like during pregnancy. After her *haflagah* has passed, she no longer has a *haflagah*. After 30 days have passed from her last period, she has no *yom hachodesh* or *onah beinonis* either. Thus, there will be no *onos* that she is required to keep.

However, until she has the status of a *zekainah*, if she does get a period, she is obligated to keep the appropriate *onos* the following month. A *zekainah* is defined by *halachah* as a woman who (a) is at the age when women usually do not object to being referred to as a *savta* (literally, grandmother) and (b) has missed her period for 90 days. Both conditions must be fulfilled.[88] If a *zekainah* were to get a period, she would not have to separate on any *onos* the following month (unless her period arrived three times).[89]

Additional Times of Required Separation in the Jewish Calendar

In addition to the separation times which we have discussed above, there are a number of other times in the Jewish year that also require a separation between husband and wife.

On *Yom Kippur*, marital relations and all affectionate contact are forbidden. In addition, all of the *harchakos* (not passing directly, sleeping in separate beds, etc.) apply as well.[90]

---

[88] *Yoreh Deah* 189:28–29. See also *Shiurei Shevet HaLevi* 189:29:3. This is probably sometime between age 60–65. The literal wording of the *Gemara* and *Shulchan Aruch* is *ima* (mother), the modern equivalent of a woman appearing old enough that someone would call her *savta*, or grandmother, by someone on the street without making her angry.

[89] *Yoreh Deah* 189: 28,30.

[90] *Orach Chayim* 615:1 and *Mishnah Berurah* ad. loc.

If either husband or wife is sitting *shivah*, marital relations are also forbidden. In addition, the accepted practice is to refrain from all forms of affectionate contact as well.[91] However, the *harchakos* do not apply during *shivah* (unless the wife is *niddah*.)[92]

Tishah B'Av also requires a separation between husband and wife. The extent of the separation is a dispute. Some authorities treat *Tishah B'Av* according to the laws of *Yom Kippur*, while others treat this day according to the laws of *shivah*.[93] One should follow the guidance of one's *halachic* authority.

---

[91] Rama, *Yoreh Deah* 383:1.

[92] *Yoreh Deah* 383.

[93] *Orach Chayim* 554:18 implies that *Tishah B'Av* is more lenient, and so rules the *Taz* 615:1. The *Machatzis Hashekel* 554:19 explains that *Yom Kippur* is stricter because women are dressed up in honor of *Yom Tov*, whereas on *Tishah B'Av* they are dressed for mourning, therefore we need not be as concerned about the *harchakos*. However, the *Darchei Moshe* 554:7 (the Rama's comments on the Tur, as opposed to his notes on *Shulchan Aruch*) states that maybe the laws of *Tishah B'Av* are the same as *Yom Kippur*; he is quoted there by *Magen Avraham*, who rules that one can be lenient in the daytime. *Mishnah Berurah* 554:37 (essentially quoting the *Darchei Moshe*) implies that one should be strict but does not rule so explicitly.

CHAPTER 11

♦

For Brides

As a *kallah*, bride, you need to be well acquainted with all the laws we have discussed in the preceding chapters. Additionally, there are special laws that concern a *kallah* before and after her wedding day. We will take a look at these special laws now.

Yichud

With the exception of close family members and certain situations,[1] the laws of *yichud*, roughly translated as "seclusion," preclude a man and woman who are not married to one another from being secluded together.[2] A bride and groom before their wedding are obligated in all the laws of *yichud*.[3] They are equally obligated in the laws of *negiyah*, which means that they are not allowed to touch each other before their wedding.[4]

Because of the challenge of keeping these laws, a bride and groom should make

---

1   There is no prohibition of *yichud* between mothers and sons, fathers and daughters (*Kiddushin* 80b), grandparents and grandchildren (*Bach Even HaEzer* 21). Brothers and sisters may be together, but should not dwell together (without other family members) for a period longer than thirty days (*Kiddushin* 81b; *Shu't Imrei Yosher* 2:43).

2   The laws of *yichud* are discussed primarily in *Kiddushin* 80b–82a and *Even HaEzer* 22.

3   As well as after the wedding in the case of *chupas niddah* (where the bride is *niddah*) or *pirsah niddah* (where the bride becomes *niddah* before marital relations take place).

4   *Shach Yoreh Deah* 157:10; 195:20.

every effort before their marriage to keep their engagement period short and not to put themselves in situations which may be tempting, for example, spending extensive periods of time together or being together late at night. The time spent together is less challenging when the couple has a purpose for being together, for example, planning the wedding, shopping for furniture or meeting each other's family members or mentors.

Setting the Wedding Date

Setting a date for your wedding can be one of the most challenging parts of your wedding preparations. Many factors can be involved in this task that may make it seem near impossible: Irregular periods, family considerations, wedding hall options to name just a few.

It is a good idea to get advice from a person knowledgeable and experienced in this area with whom you are comfortable to help you set the date.

Avoiding Chupas Niddah

Some women choose to take synthetic hormones to avoid being *niddah* on their wedding day. This practice is allowed by *halachah*, but it is not required. However, if a *kallah* chooses this option, it is extremely important that the correct type of pill is taken.

For the purpose of pushing off a period to avoid *chupas niddah*, only the hormone progestin is needed and in a dosage that is 1/8 to 1/4 the dosage of the amount in a normal birth control pill. This type of pill can be used for at least two weeks for the purpose of pushing off her upcoming period.[5] (This pill, which is not a contraceptive, is also used to treat women with heavy periods, irregular periods, women who do not ovulate regularly and women with endometriosis.)

Although no hormonal treatment that alters a woman's natural cycle is without problems, the progestin-only pill has been proven effective in the vast majority of cases, with fewer problems of break-through bleeding and negative side

---

[5] Medical personnel note that this pill can be used longer with no adverse side effects, however, it may not push a period off more than two weeks.

effects than other pills, if used properly. (Its efficacy depends on following spe-cific instructions for usage.) If you are interested in a hormonal treatment to avoid being *niddah* on your wedding day, consult a *halachic* authority as well as a doctor who is well versed in this area.

Doctors or other practitioners often mistakenly prescribe regular birth con-trol pills (in contraceptive doses) to regulate a *kallah*'s period. These pills nor-mally contain both estrogen and progestin, and are recommended for a minimum of three months time. A major *halachic* and practical problem for a *kallah* using these pills is the significantly increased risk of miscarriage afterwards (which is why another form of birth control is often recommended for use the first month after a woman stops taking this type of pill).

Before the Wedding

Before the wedding, as a *kallah*, you will need to complete the entire *taharah* process. This means making a successful *hefsek taharah*, counting the Seven Clean Days, preparing for and going to the *mikveh*. (See Ch. 6, 7 and 8 for the details involved in this process.)

Normally, a woman must wait a minimum of five days from the beginning of her bleeding before counting the Seven Clean Days. However, a *kallah* before her wedding does not need to wait the usual five days before counting the Seven Clean Days if her period (or any other bleeding from the uterus) lasts less than five days.[6]

The Taharah Process

Every *kallah*,[7] needs to complete the following three steps:

◆ Step One: Make a *hefsek taharah*;

---

[6]   *Taz Yoreh Deah* 196:7. *Shach Yoreh Deah* 196:20 rules this way only under extenuating circum-stances, for example, if otherwise it will result in a *chupas niddah*.

[7]   This is required whether or not a bride has ever had a period or she is post-menopausal and is now remarrying (*Pischei Teshuvah* 192:2), due to the concern that the desire for married life might cause a spot of uterine blood.

- Step Two: Count the Seven Clean Days, making the necessary *bedikos*; and

- Step Three: Immerse in a *mikveh*.

We will now discuss each of these steps with the special details that apply to brides.

Step One:
Making the Hefsek Taharah

As we learned, the *hefsek taharah* is the special, internal check that is made to ascertain that all the bleeding from your period (or any other uterine bleeding) has indeed stopped. Making the *hefsek taharah* is an absolute *halachic* precondition to be able to count the Seven Clean Days.[8]

It is a good idea to review the procedure for making a *hefsek taharah* that we discussed in Chapter 6. As a *kallah*, you are not required to make this internal check too deeply, if you are not able.[9] Similarly, you may be unable to make a proper *moch*.

You will need to make your *hefsek taharah* a minimum of eight days before the day of your wedding to be able to immerse in the *mikveh* the night before your wedding.

If you are only able to make your *hefsek* seven days before the wedding, a *kallah* is allowed to go to the *mikveh* during the daytime of the seventh clean day, as long as the wedding will take place after nightfall.[10]

Some communities prefer a *kallah* to immerse during the daytime (either on

---

[8]   *Yoreh Deah* 196:1.

[9]   *Sidrei Taharah* 196:23 s.v. *uvihachi*. This applies to a *kallah* who is a *besulah* (virgin), since she may injure herself.

[10] Ordinarily a woman may not go to *mikveh* during the daytime (*Yoreh Deah* 197:3). The reason is so that she won't make a mistake and go on the seventh day and subsequently have relations before nightfall. However, a *kallah* may go to the *mikveh* during the daytime (Rama, *Yoreh Deah* 197:3). Many *poskim* only permit a *kallah* to go during the daytime after the seventh day but not on the seventh day (*Shach Yoreh Deah* 197:9). The prevalent practice, however, is to permit immersing on the seventh day for a *kallah*, provided the *chupah* is after nightfall (*Dagul Mei'Revavah* ad loc.).

the eighth day or on the seventh day if the *chupah* will be after nightfall, as we discussed), so that the *mikveh* attendant can spend more time explaining the procedures to her. Since *mikveh* houses are not open during the day, it will be necessary to make special arrangements if you are immersing during the daytime.

In addition, many *mikveh* houses prefer to be told in advance that a *kallah* is coming. That way, they can make an appointment for you, make sure you have the nicest room and be able to spend more time with you.

If possible, it is a good idea to try to make your *hefsek* a few days earlier than necessary. This way, if a question arises about any color you may find on your *bedikah* cloth, it can be answered without anxiety.

Step Two:
Counting the Seven Clean Days

On each of the Seven Clean Days, make one *bedikah* in the morning after sunrise and another before sunset. You may want to review the section in Chapter 6, *Making Bedikos Easier*. If making the *bedikos* is difficult or painful, or if you suspect in any way that the *bedikos* are causing bleeding, consult your *kallah* teacher and/ or your *halachic* authority.

Step Three:
Immersing in the Mikveh

The best time to immerse in the *mikveh* is as close to the wedding as possible.[11] However, if circumstances do not allow, you may go to the *mikveh* earlier. In this case, you will need to continue making *bedikos* (one a day) if four or more days will pass until marital relations take place.[12]

---

[11]   Rama, *Yoreh Deah* 192:2.
[12]   Rama, *Yoreh Deah* 192:2, since the emotional desire for relations could cause a tiny amount of *niddah* bleeding. Some authorities (*Bach* 192 s.v. *kasav bihagahos maamonis*; *Sidrei Taharah* 192:8; *Chochmas Adam* 115:3) require a *kallah* to make one *bedikah* every day from the completion of her Seven Clean Days until the marriage is consummated. Rama holds that this is necessary only if four days (or more) will intervene between the completion of the Seven Clean Days and the consummation of the marriage.

A *kallah* is permitted to go to the *mikveh motzaei Shabbos* (the night after *Shabbos*), even if she is not getting married that night or Sunday night.[13]

If you are getting married on a Sunday night, the best time to immerse is Sunday during the daytime (if it is the community's custom for a *kallah* to immerse during the daytime); otherwise, *motzaei Shabbos* is the next most preferable time, followed by Friday during the daytime or Thursday night, if necessary.[14]

The Wedding Day

The day of your wedding can be one of the most powerful days of your life.

For the entire day and particularly under the *chupah*, both the bride and the groom are endowed with a special connection to *Hashem*. It is the time to pray intensely both for yourself and for others in need.[15]

The wedding day also has the potential to bring complete forgiveness for all your previous wrongdoings.[16] In this sense, it is likened to a private *Yom Kippur*.[17] Because of this, there is a custom to fast on the wedding day.[18] If you do not fast well or are not feeling well, you are not required to fast.[19] In addition, there are certain days in the Jewish calendar when the *choson* (groom) and *kallah* do not fast. These days are:

---

[13] *Pischei Teshuvah* 197:7, quoting *Shu't Noda BiYehudah Yoreh Deah* 117. It is best to make preparations for the *mikveh* as close as possible to immersion. Regarding preparing and immersing on *motzaei Shabbos*: The reason this is not ideal for a married woman is due to the possibility that when preparing entirely after nightfall, a woman might be tempted to rush through her preparations. However, this reason does not apply to a *kallah* unless she is getting married Saturday night. Therefore a *kallah* may plan her *tevilah* for *motzaei Shabbos*.

[14] Rama, *Yoreh Deah* 192:2.

[15] *Shelah, Shaar HaOsiyos, Os Kuf* s.v. *utzrichin hachoson*; *Kitzur Shulchan Aruch* 146:4.

[16] See *Yevamos* 63b and *yerushalmi Bikurim* 3:3 (in reference to the *choson*). See the *Tashbeitz* of Rav Shimshon bar Tzadok 465 (in reference to the *kallah*). This is also implied by *Magen Avraham* 573: intro.

[17] *Shu't Mahari Bruno* 93; *Shu't Maharam Mintz* 109.

[18] Rama, *Orach Chayim* 562:2; *Even HaEzer* 61:1. Not all *Sefardim* have this custom (see *Sdei Chemed* vol. 7 pg. 15; *Shu't Yabia Omer* 3:*Even HaEzer*:9:5; *Nisuin KeHilchasah* pg. 198).

[19] *Aruch HaShulchan, Even HaEzer* 61:21.

◆ *Rosh Chodesh*[20] with the exception of some authorities who rule that a *choson* and *kallah* should fast on *Rosh Chodesh Nisan;*[21]

◆ All the days of *Chanukah;*[22]

◆ *Isru Chag* (the day after *Sukkos, Pesach* and *Shavuos*);[23]

◆ *Tu B'Shevat* and *Tu B'Av;*[24]

◆ *Purim;*[25] *Shushan Purim* and *Purim Katan* (the 14th and 15th day of *Adar I*).[26]

On other days when *Tachanun* is not said, such as the entire month of *Nisan*, *Lag B'Omer*, the first days of *Sivan* before *Shavuos* (and a week after *Shavuos* as well in Israel) and the days between *Yom Kippur* and *Sukkos*, the prevailing custom is for the *choson* and *kallah* to fast.[27]

Even if you are not fasting, you should not drink alcoholic beverages the entire day.[28] If the wedding is after nightfall, many *halachic* authorities rule that you may break your fast at the end of the Jewish day (before the *chupah*).[29]

Because your wedding day is likened to a private *Yom Kippur*, additional prayers

---

[20]   *Taz* 573:1.

[21]   The dispute about fasting on *Rosh Chodesh Nisan* is discussed in *Magen Avraham* and *Pri Megadim* 580. Those who rule that one should fast on *Rosh Chodesh Nisan* base their ruling on the fact that there are certain days that are called *ta'aniyos tzadikim*, "fast of righteous people." In earlier generations, great *tzadikim* fasted on these days, the dates of which are recorded in *Orach Chayim* 580.

[22]   Rama, *Orach Chayim* 573:1.

[23]   *Magen Avraham* 573:1.

[24]   Ibid.

[25]   *Mishnah Berurah* 573:6.

[26]   *Orach Chayim* 697:1.

[27]   *Mishnah Berurah* 573:7 and *Magen Avraham* 573:1. *Eliyahu Rabbah* 573:3 quotes *Nachalas Shivah* that they do not fast any day that one does not recite *Tachanun*. However, *Aishel Avraham* (ad loc.) points out that the custom is that they do fast on these days.

[28]   *Aruch HaShulchan, Even HaEzer* 44:4.

[29]   See *Pischei Teshuvah* 61:9 and *Chochmas Adam* 129:2; *Kitzur Shulchan Aruch* 146:1. *Aruch HaShulchan, Even HaEzer* 61:21 rules that the *choson* and *kallah* fast until the *chupah*.

are said during the day, including the confessional prayer called *Vidui*.[30] These additions can be found in the afternoon service before *Yom Kippur*. If you are fasting, the prayer aneinu ("answer us") is also added to your *Amidah* prayer.[31]

As with the days leading up to *Yom Kippur*, what you can accomplish spiritually on your wedding day depends on how much you have prepared beforehand. Amidst all the excitement that goes along with a wedding, as well as all the preparations that need to be made in the physical world, is the enormous spiritual potential of the day.

As a *kallah*, take the time to look inside yourself. Decide what you would like to change. Examine the underlying reasons behind any negative behavior and make a concrete plan for self-improvement. Ask *Hashem* on your wedding day for forgiveness for your past wrongdoings and for the strength in the future to implement your plan and become a better person.

A Bride Who Is Niddah on the Wedding Day

Every woman tries her utmost to plan the date of her wedding carefully to make sure she will not be *niddah* on her wedding day. However, as much as we plan, it can happen — and it is not uncommon.

If you are not able to complete the Seven Clean Days or your period arrives a few days before the wedding day, you will, of course, feel disappointed. Now is the time to stay focused on the positive: *Hashem* is giving you a wonderful husband with whom you will, God willing, spend the rest of your life. Being physically separate on the day of the wedding and/or during any *Sheva Brachos* (the seven festive days of meals after the wedding) can allow you and your husband to focus on the inspiring spirituality of these special days.

What changes can you expect if you are *niddah*? The wedding can take place

---

[30] Rama, *Orach Chayim* 562:2). Not all *Sefardim* follow this custom (see *Sdei Chemed* 7:16).
[31] Rama, *Orach Chayim* 562:2.

as scheduled. A few changes will also be necessary in the ceremony and after-wards, all of which can be done with the utmost discretion.

Some *halachic* authorities require that when your *choson* puts the ring on your finger, instead of sliding it on, he should try to place it on top of your finger.[32] However, many prominent authorities allow the *choson* to put the ring on the *kallah*'s finger, taking care not to touch.[33] After the *chupah*, many authorities are of the opinion that all the *harchakos* (not passing directly to one another, etc.) apply.[34]

Until you have immersed in the *mikveh*, you and your husband are not allowed to be completely alone together. Since you may not be secluded together, there are a number of different options for the *yichud* room (the room where a couple is alone together after the ceremony). The witnesses to the *yichud* will need to be aware of the situation so arrangements can be made. Discuss with your *halachic* authority which option is most comfortable for you.

You also will have to make special sleeping arrangements during the night (or nights). Here, there are also a number of options available, including staying at a hotel in separate rooms or with friends. Again, discuss with your *halachic* authority which option is most comfortable for you.[35]

Pirsah Niddah

If the *kallah* becomes *niddah* after the *chupah*, but before the couple has experi-

---

[32] *Maharil* quoted by *Ba'er Heiteiv Even HaEzer* 61:8.

[33] *Ba'er Heiteiv Even HaEzer* 61:8; *Shu't Binyan Tziyon* 139; *Darchei Teshuvah* 195:13.

[34] Ibid.

[35] Regarding this situation, the wording found in the *Shulchan Aruch* (*Even HaEzer* 22:1; *Yoreh Deah* 383:2 and 192:4) quotes the *Gemara* (*Kesubos* 4a), which says, literally, "He sleeps among the men, and she sleeps among the women." There are thus disputes about what this term means. The general assumption is that it refers to a situation where they are sleeping in a large room where other men and women sleeping (a situation which we would not find today). There is a wide range of opinions among the *poskim* as to how this translates into practice. The Chazon Ish rules that they are allowed to sleep in the same room (without chaperons) as long as there is another couple in the house and the bedroom doors are slightly open (*Devar Halachah* pg. 86).

enced marital relations, the couple also may not be secluded together. In this case, the same *halachos* apply as in a *chupas niddah*.[36]

If the couple has experienced incomplete marital relations or have abstained by choice, and the *kallah* becomes *niddah*, a question should be asked to their *halachic* authority as to whether or not they may be completely alone together.[37]

Marital Relations for the First Time and Afterwards

A number of special *halachos* apply when a woman experiences marital relations for the first time.[38] These laws do not apply to women who have previously experienced marital relations.

A woman who experiences relations for the first time becomes *niddah*. This special type of *niddah*[39] applies after the first time a woman experiences complete

---

36 *Yoreh Deah* 192:4.

37 Regarding willful abstention, Rama, *Yoreh Deah* 192:4 rules that *yichud* is allowed. *Taz* ad loc., 192:7 disagrees with Rama and prohibits *yichud* in this case. *Shiurei Shevet HaLevi* 192:4 rules like *Taz*.

38 There is a disagreement between *halachic* authorities as to whether or not these laws apply to a woman who has never had marital relations but has had her hymen surgically removed. There is also a dispute regarding a situation as to whether or not a woman whose hymen is surgically removed after her marriage is rendered *niddah*. Rav Moshe Feinstein (*Igros Moshe Yoreh Deah* 1:87) contends that the law that a woman is a *niddah* from *dam besulim* (which is a *takanas chachomim*) was instituted only when the *besulim* are broken by relations. Other *halachic* authorities contend that Chazal ruled that the *besulim* are considered *niddah* *miderabbanan* regardless of why they were removed or bled (*Maharsham* 1:210; *Shu't Minchas Yitzchak* 4:58; *Badei HaShulchan* 193:2).

39 The reason our Sages enacted this rabbinical form of *niddah* is because there might be some undetected *niddah* blood that leaves the woman at the same time that the hymen is bleeding (*Rosh Kesubos* 1:9). Even in the case where blood is not seen, we assume that there was probably a small amount of blood that was covered by the seed (*Yoreh Deah* 193:1). Rashba (quoted by *Beis Yosef* 193) asks why, then, aren't we concerned every time a woman has a wound in the vaginal area that maybe some undetected *niddah* blood mixed in with the wound? He answers that, even though we should be stringent, if we were, then a woman who has irritations in the vaginal area would no longer be able to remain married. Therefore our Sages applied this ruling only for a *besulah* (a temporary situation), but did not extend it to a woman who has wounds.

marital relations whether or not there is blood, or even if relations are not complete, but she sees blood.[40]

The *halachic* process is as follows: Following the couple's first marital relations, they separate. (They do not need to do so immediately but may wait until the husband's body naturally separates from his wife.[41])

This special category of *niddah* due to *dam besulim* (blood from the hymen) requires a wait of only four days (instead of the usual five) before making a *hefsek taharah* and counting the Seven Clean Days.[42] The first of these four days is the (Jewish) day in which the relations took place. Thus the check of *hefsek taharah* can be made before sunset on the fourth day instead of before sunset on the fifth day.

If the woman gets her period during these first four days, the normal laws of *niddah* apply, and she must wait five days before counting the Seven Clean Days. However, the days she has already waited after having relations can be counted toward the five days in a case where the woman's period lasts less than five days.[43]

Similarly, if she is in the middle of her *taharah* from *dam besulim* and gets her period during her Seven Clean Days, she need only wait until her period is over before making her *hefsek taharah*, if her period lasts less than five days.

It is normal for a couple who has never experienced marital relations before to approach intimacy slowly. It is also normal (and common) for most new couples not to experience complete marital relations the first time (or times) that they are intimate.[44] However, relations that are incomplete may nevertheless

---

[40]   Rama, *Yoreh Deah* 193.

[41]   *Yoreh Deah* 193 with *Taz* (1) and *Shach* (1). Even if there is blood flowing from the hymen, they may complete relations in a normal manner.

[42]   *Taz* 193:4.

[43]   For example, a woman who has already been separate from her husband for two days gets her period, which lasts for only three days. At the end of the third day of her period, before sunset, she may make her *hefsek taharah*, since she and her husband would have been separate the required total of five days before beginning the count of the Seven Clean Days.

[44]   If relations have not been completed and the *kallah* is not *niddah*, some couples feel more comfortable acting as if they are *niddah* in public after the wedding night to preserve their privacy.

render a woman *niddah*. Questions may need to be asked and can be done without embarrassment. It is important that the *choson* establish a relationship with a Rav with whom he feels comfortable to ask any question that may arise.

Many *halachic* authorities rule that the *kallah* does not need to check for blood on the second time she and her husband have complete relations and thereafter.[45] However, if blood is found, the *kallah* again becomes *niddah* and follows the same procedure as discussed above for *dam besulim* (that is, she counts four and then seven days before going to the *mikveh* unless her period arrives during this time).

If a woman experiences pain or discomfort during the second or subsequent marital relations, which is common, many *halachic* authorities rule that she is not required to check for blood or do a *bedikah*.[46]

Problems with discomfort and blood, although normal during the beginning of a couple's intimate life, can be helped with a water-soluble form of lubrication.[47]

Establishing Normal Relations

Once marital relations take place without pain or blood, some *halachic* authorities rule that a woman with a *halachically* irregular period needs to make a series of three *bedikos* following marital relations to establish that relations do not bring on *niddah* blood (an extremely rare condition).[48]

For the *bedikos* to fulfill this requirement, they must be made at a time when a period is expected to arrive. There are differences in opinion as to when this time falls out in a woman's cycle. Thus, if you have a *halachically* irregular period (see Ch. 10 for definitions), ask a question to your *halachic* authority if these *bedikos* need to be made, and if so, when is the proper time to make them.

---

45 See *Badei HaShulchan* 193 *Biurim* s.v. im ba. However, *Taharas HaBayis* 1:509 implies that she must make a *bedikah*. *Aruch HaShulchan* 193:11 rules that she should check the sheets for blood.

46 *Shu't Minchas Yitzchak* 5:61 and *Darchei Teshuvah* 193:3. However, *Shiurei Shevet HaLevi* 193: end of 7 rules that if she experiences pain, she must check for blood.

47 Such as K-Y Jelly or the like.

48 Whether or not these *bedikos* need to be made is a dispute between *Shach* (who rules that they do not need to be made) and the *Shulchan Aruch* (*Yoreh Deah* 186:2). Most authorities rule like the *Shulchan Aruch* (that these *bedikos* should be made), but Rav Moshe Feinstein (*Igros Moshe Yoreh Deah* 2:75) rules like *Shach* that there is no requirement.

CHAPTER 12

♦

Pregnancy, Birth and Afterwards

In this chapter, we will discuss the laws that are relevant to a woman when she is pregnant, while giving birth and during the months after birth.

Pregnancy and Onos

A Woman Who Has a Halachically Irregular Period

Most women find out they are pregnant after they miss their first period. For the majority of women who have *halachically* irregular periods, this will mean that they will have observed their separation *onos* (see Ch. 10) — the *yom hachodesh*, *haflagah* and *beinonis* — the first month of their pregnancy. Once these *onos* pass with no bleeding or period, they are henceforth uprooted, meaning there is no longer any obligation to separate the next month.[1]

If you have a *halachically* irregular period and find out you are pregnant before your *onos* pass, most authorities rule that you are still obligated to keep these separation times the first month.[2]

---

[1]   For a *halachically* irregular period, the *haflagah* and *beinonis* are measured only from the last period, which in this case, was skipped. The *yom hachodesh* is cancelled after the first time the date arrived without a period.

[2]   *Yoreh Deah* 184:7, 34. Rav Moshe Feinstein (*Igros Moshe Yoreh Deah* 3:52) disagrees and rules that the separation *onos* need not be observed if the pregnancy is medically confirmed. For a lengthy discussion of this topic, see Rav Eliyahu Falk, *Machazeh Eliyahu*, Ch. 105, and his

A Woman Who Has a Halachically Regular Period

A woman who has an active *veses kavua* (*halachically* regular period) is required to observe her regular separation *onah* (or *onos*) for the first three months of the pregnancy, according to most authorities.[3]

Bleeding During Pregnancy

Women often bleed or spot during pregnancy. Some women even see a light period, particularly during the first three months. Any time a woman sees blood during a pregnancy, she should be in touch with her doctor, even though the bleeding might not indicate anything serious.

As with any time a woman sees blood at a time when she is not expecting her period, she should try to ascertain (through her doctor or her *niddah* nurse) the source of the bleeding, then discuss this information with her *halachic* authority.

In addition, during pregnancy there are certain changes in the laws of *vesasos* (the required separation times the following month), which we will discuss below. It is important to note that if a woman becomes *niddah* during pregnancy, all the normal laws of *niddah* apply. That is, the husband and wife must separate, the wife makes her *hefsek taharah* a minimum of five days after the bleeding began (if possible), she then counts the Seven Clean Days, prepares and immerses in a *mikveh*.

Bleeding or Staining During Pregnancy for a Woman Who Has a Halachically Irregular Period: Onah Requirements

If a woman bleeds (*niddah* blood) during the first three months of pregnancy,

---

sources there, including: *Midrash Rabbah* (*Parshas Tazria* 14:3), *Shu't Chasam Sofer Yoreh Deah* 169, *Shu't Avodas HaGershuni* 21, *Shu't Rabbi Akiva Eiger* 128; and *Shu't Avnei Nezer Yoreh Deah* 238:3.

3   *Yoreh Deah* 184:7. See ftn. 2 above.

and she has a *halachically* irregular period, then the next month all the regular separation *onos* are kept.[4]

If she bleeds (*niddah* blood) after the first three months of pregnancy, only the *onos* of the *yom hachodesh* and *haflagah* (if relevant) are kept the following month.[5] (There will only be a *haflagah* if she bled two or more times after the first three months of pregnancy.) She is not required to separate on the *beinonis*.[6]

A *niddah*-colored stain (*kesem*) that renders a woman *niddah* does not usually count for *vesasos* (and hence, there are no separation *onos* based on this the following month). However, if a *niddah*-colored stain is found on a *bedikah* cloth, then the separation *onos* are usually required (in addition to all the laws of *niddah*). If you stain during pregnancy, check with your *halachic* authority if you are required to observe any *onos* the following month.[7]

Bleeding or Staining During Pregnancy for a Woman Who Has a Halachically Regular Period: Onah Requirements

If a woman bleeds (*niddah* blood) during the first three months of pregnancy, most *halachic* authorities rule that the normal *onos* are kept the following month.[8]

After the first three months, all *niddah* bleeding is treated by the same laws as

---

[4]   *Yoreh Deah* 189:34. For those who follow Rav Moshe Feinstein's opinion, only the *yom hachodesh* and *haflagah* would be required (*Yoreh Deah* 3:52).

[5]   *Yoreh Deah* 189:33 and *Pischei Teshuvah* 189:31.

[6]   *Shiurei Shevet HaLevi* 189:33:5.

[7]   *Yoreh Deah* 190:54. The *Shulchan Aruch* rules that *vesasos* are required from blood on a *bedikah* cloth but not from a *kesem*. *Shiurei Shevet HaLevi* 190:54:7 writes that blood on a *bedikah* does not necessarily count towards a *veses*. *Igros Moshe Yoreh Deah* 3:51 rules that if a woman stains before her period (the flow) starts, she should count from the staining, but *only if* she usually does not sense when her period starts or if three times in a row she stained before her period started (even if she usually senses when her period starts). However, if there is a day's interruption when there was neither staining nor flow, Rav Moshe Feinstein rules that one counts the *veses* from the flow, not from the previous staining.

[8]   *Yoreh Deah* 189:33, 44.

those for a *halachically* irregular period during pregnancy, which means, she is obligated to separate the next month on the *yom hachodesh* and the *haflagah* (if relevant) the following month.[9] (There will only be a *haflagah* if she bled two or more times after the first three months of pregnancy.) There is no requirement to separate on the *beinonis*.[10]

Even if the bleeding occurs three times in a row in a pattern of a *halachically* regular period, a woman who is pregnant cannot establish a *veses kavua*.[11] Instead, the bleeding is treated as *veses she'ayno kavua*, which requires the *onos* of the *yom hachodesh* and *haflagah* (if relevant) to be observed the following month but not the *beinonis*.[12]

A *niddah*-colored stain (*kesem*) that renders a woman *niddah* does not usually count for *vesasos* (and hence, there are no separation *onos* based on this the following month). However, if a *niddah*-colored stain is found on a *bedikah* cloth, then the separation *onos* are usually required (in addition to all the laws of *niddah*). If you stain during pregnancy, check with your *halachic* authority if you are required to observe any *onos* the following month.[13]

Bleeding During Pregnancy From Doctors' Visits

For most women, an internal examination by a doctor during pregnancy (especially in the ninth month) will cause the vaginal tissue to bleed. Although the blood is almost always not *niddah* blood, but rather *dam makeh* (blood from a wound), it is important to discuss this issue with and receive guidelines from your *halachic* authority before a doctor's visit, so that you do not become *niddah* unnecessarily.

---

9   *Yoreh Deah* 189:33 and *Pischei Teshuvah* 189:31.
10   *Shiurei Shevet HaLevi* 189:33:5.
11   *Yoreh Deah* 189:33.
12   *Yoreh Deah* 189:34, *Shiurei Shevet HaLevi* 189:33(5).
13   *Yoreh Deah* 190:54. See ftn. 7 above.

Childbirth — When Does a Woman Become Niddah?

When the Water Breaks

The sac that holds the amniotic fluid can break before the onset of labor, at the beginning stages of labor or not at all until the baby is being born. Many *halachic* authorities rule that the flow of this fluid at the beginning of labor (or before) — when contractions are still several minutes apart — does not render a woman *niddah* if it is not accompanied by blood.[14]

However, if the sac breaks while you are in active labor,[15] and it appears that birth is imminent, many authorities rule that you and your husband should separate.[16]

Losing the Mucous Plug

During pregnancy, an outer layer, or "plug," of mucous covers the cervix. The plug can come out during birth, although sometimes it comes out much earlier — even days or weeks before birth. You may or may not notice when the plug comes out. When the plug comes out, it can be tinged with blood (what is called "the bloody show" by medical personnel). There is a disagreement among *halachic* authorities as to whether or not the passing of this mucous plug renders a woman *niddah*, even in cases where the plug is tinged with blood.[17] Consult with your *halachic* authority if you see that your mucous plug has passed.

Membrane Stripping

This is a procedure that doctors or midwives sometimes perform for the pur-

---

[14] Responsum from Rav Shlomo Zalman Auerbach printed in *Marei Kohen* pg. 184.

[15] Meaning, the contractions are close together or the woman is in the stage of labor called "transition," (which usually means a seven to ten centimeter dilation).

[16] *Shiurei Shevet HaLevi* 194:2:4 s.v. *ubiyeridas*. Here Rav Wosner also says the couple should stay separate if the active labor stops.

[17] Some authorities contend that that the passing of the mucous plug (even with blood) does not render a woman *niddah*, since it is considered blood from a wound. See Rabbi Binyomin Forst, *Laws of Niddah*, Vol. I, pg. 465. Others disagree. See *Shiurei Shevet HaLevi* 194:2:4 at the end.

pose of hastening labor. Membrane stripping separates the sac that holds the amniotic fluid from the uterine wall. When done quickly, it can be extremely painful and traumatic, however, when done slowly and carefully, it need not be painful and is equally effective. A woman should make a point to inform her practitioner that, before performing this procedure, she should be asked.

Some authorities rule that even if no blood is found, the woman is rendered *niddah* by this procedure due to the principle of *pesichas hakever* (there is no opening of the womb without blood, even if no blood was found).[18] Others rule differently. A couple should consult their *halachic* authority on this matter.

Bleeding

Labor, at any stage can be accompanied by a flow of fresh, bright-red blood. This type of bleeding renders a woman *niddah*.[19]

Dilation

When a woman is fully dilated and in active labor, birth is usually imminent. If a woman has not become *niddah* until this point, she and her husband must separate, since she will become *niddah* at any moment.[20] However, partial dilation of the cervix in the earlier stages of labor does not, in and of itself, render a woman *niddah*.[21]

"On the Delivery Stool"

This is a concept in *halachah* that connotes a time when the labor has become so strong that the woman can no longer walk (in between contractions). This can occur during what is called "transition." If a woman has not become *niddah* until this point, she and her husband should separate.[22]

---

[18] *Niddah* 21a.
[19] *Yoreh Deah* 194:1.3.
[20] *Sidrei Taharah* 194:25.
[21] *Igros Moshe Yoreh Deah* 2:76; *Shiurei Shevet HaLevi* 194:2(4).
[22] *Sidrei Taharah* 194:25.

Husband Attending the Delivery

Most *halachic* authorities permit the husband to be present at the delivery of his child.[23] For many women, their husband's presence lends necessary emotional support during the difficult moments of childbirth. However, once a woman becomes *niddah* during childbirth, all the normal *halachos* of *niddah* apply. For example, they may not touch and the husband may not see any part of his wife's body that is normally covered. For this reason, there are a number of hospitals in Israel that do not allow a husband to be in the room with his wife during the birth. If you are planning to give birth in Israel and would like to have your husband with you through the birth, ask the hospital beforehand as to its policy regarding this issue.

After Birth

The *Torah* requires a woman to separate from her husband after natural (vaginal) childbirth for seven days if the newborn child is a boy and for fourteen days for a girl.[24]

However, since the practice to treat all uterine blood[25] as *zavah* blood became *halachah*,[26] we now wait until all the bleeding after childbirth has stopped, make a *hefsek taharah*, count the Seven Clean Days and then immerse in the *mikveh*.

After childbirth, women normally bleed for three to eight weeks. During the initial week (or weeks, if possible) after birth, it is important for a woman to rest to properly heal from the birth. In addition, rest is almost always a necessary

---

23 *Igros Moshe Yoreh Deah* II:75. Those who rule otherwise include *Shiurei Shevet HaLevi* 195:7:3 s.v. *bizman* who rules that he can be in the labor room but not in the delivery room. *Nishmas Avraham Yoreh Deah* 195:3 quotes *Shu't Minchas Yitzchak* and Rav Henkin that the husband should not attend the delivery unless there is a *pikuach nefashos* situation. Rav Shlomo Zalman Auerbach (quoted in *Nishmas Avraham*, Vol. 2, pg. 108) rules that although it is technically permitted for the husband to attend, he strongly advises against it.

24 *Vayikra* 23:1–5.

25 From the shedding of the lining of the uterus.

26 See Rama, *Yoreh Deah* 196:11.

component of a positive emotional state and can significantly hasten the end of the bleeding after birth.

Miscarriage

In the unfortunate event that a woman experiences a miscarriage, the same laws apply as after birth (see above), with the following exceptions: If the pregnancy was less than 40 days (measuring from conception, not the last period), the *Torah* requirement that a woman must separate from her husband seven days for a boy and fourteen days for a girl does not apply.[27] This would mean that a woman could make her *hefsek taharah* after five days (if the bleeding had stopped) and then proceed to count her Seven Clean Days and immerse in the *mikveh* afterwards.

If the pregnancy was more than 40 days (counting from conception), and the sex of the fetus was not known or a female, the woman must wait a minimum of fourteen days (total) before immersing in the *mikveh*.[28] During this time, she may make her *hefsek taharah* and count the Seven Clean Days. However, if she finishes her Seven Clean Days on the 12th or 13th day after the miscarriage, she must wait until the night after the 14th day to immerse in the *mikveh*.

If the pregnancy was more than 40 days (counting from conception) and the sex of the fetus was known to be a male, she may immerse in the *mikveh* immediately after her Seven Clean Days.

Resuming Vesasos

The bleeding that accompanies childbirth and afterwards is not considered a period. Even though it is *niddah* blood (which requires the proper *taharah* process), no separation *onos* are calculated based on the onset of bleeding from childbirth.[29]

---

[27] *Yoreh Deah* 194:2.
[28] If the sex of the fetus was known, she follows the procedure for after birth as we discussed above.
[29] *Badei HaShulchan, Biurim* 189:33.

For the first 24 months after a woman gives birth, she has the status of a *meinekes*, a nursing mother (whether she is nursing her baby or not during this time).[30] The Sages in the *Gemara* ruled that a woman's period was unlikely to resume for these first 24 months since her body was recuperating from child-birth. Thus, since she needn't be concerned that her period would begin during this time, the *rishonim* rule that she was exempt from previously existing *vesasos*[31] and, moreover, cannot establish a *veses kavua* during the same time period.[32] A minority opinion in the *Gemara*[33] contends that the reason a woman's period didn't resume during this time was due to the child being nursed for these 24 months,[34] as was encouraged.[35]

In our day, since most women's periods resume much earlier than 24 months after giving birth (even when nursing), most contemporary *halachic* authorities rule that the laws of *vesasos* begin once a woman's period resumes.[36] For a woman who had a *veses she'ayna kavua* before her pregnancy, the calculations of her separation *onos* begin anew and are not carried over from before the pregnancy.[37]

A woman who had an active *veses kavua* before she became pregnant should consult her *halachic* authority if her period resumes within 24 months after giving birth to ascertain whether or not her *veses kavua* is active again or whether it is only considered active after 24 months.

---

[30] *Niddah* 9a.
[31] The *rishonim* follow the Sages and rule that her concern for her *veses* is only after 24 months have transpired whether or not she is nursing (*Yoreh Deah* 189:7, 34).
[32] *Yoreh Deah* 189:33. Even if she experienced three cycles in a row in a pattern of a *veses kavua*, each was treated as a *veses she'ayna kavua*, since each period was considered an aberration.
[33] *Niddah* 9a.
[34] Thus, if a woman was not nursing, she should expect her period to resume.
[35] See *Pischei Teshuvah Yoreh Deah* 81:16. *Kesubos* 39a and *Yevamos* 12b show us that it was normative at the time for a baby to be nursed for 18–24 months, and they imply that a significant amount of the baby's nutrition came from his mother during that time.
[36] *Igros Moshe Yoreh Deah* 3:52; *Marei Kohen* pg.161. See also *Shiurei Shevet HaLevi* 184:7(4). See also the discussion in *Tosafos Chadashim, Niddah* 1:4; *Shu't Chasam Sofer Yoreh Deah* 70, and *Lechem V'Simlah, Simlah* 189:54.
[37] Since they were uprooted by the pregnancy, according to the opinion of the majority of *poskim*. See *Shiurei Shevet HaLevi* 189:34.

Many women find that in the first weeks (even months) after birth, hormonal fluctuations as well as adjustments in a baby's nursing schedule can cause *niddah* bleeding. A woman in this situation should consult her *halachic* authority as to her requirements regarding *onos*.

CHAPTER 13

♦

Birth Control

Jewish law allows the use of birth control in situations where it would be dangerous to have a child — such as when pregnancy or birth would be physically or emotionally dangerous for the mother.[1]

In this chapter, we will discuss a summary of the *mitzvos* and *halachos* involved in the use of birth control. This discussion is meant only as an introduction to the many issues involved. Every decision to use birth control must be made on an individual basis in consultation with a *halachic* authority.

Positive Commandments

The use of birth control involves foregoing a number of positive *mitzvos*. The decision to use birth control must be made with an understanding of the central importance in Judaism of these *mitzvos*.

The positive *Torah* commandment, *pru urvu*, "be fruitful and multiply," was given to Adam and Eve in the Garden of Eden.[2] Technically, only the husband has a *mitzvah* of *pru urvu*,[3] and he fulfills this obligation by fathering one boy and one

---

[1] *Yevamos* 12b; *Kesubos* 39a.
[2] *Bereishis* 1:28.
[3] *Even HaEzer* 1:13.

girl.[4] However, when a woman agrees to marriage, she is *halachically* obligated to help her husband fulfill this *mitzvah*.[5]

Moreover, he may not release her of this obligation.[6]

Further, in regards to the obligation to bear children, there are two other on-going *mitzvos*. So important are these *mitzvos* that each is referred to as a *mitzvah rabbah*, a "great commandment."[7]

The first of these *mitzvos* has its source in the book of *Yeshayahu* (Isaiah), where the prophet tells us, "God ... created it (the earth) not in vain; He formed it to be inhabited,"[8] meaning that populating the world is considered part of our God-given mission. This task is also part of what our mystical tradition, the *Kabbalah*, calls *tikun olam*, a term which refers to our job of "fixing the world" after mankind's sin in the Garden of Eden.[9] This *mitzvah* of populating the world is referred to in Hebrew as *lasheves*, "to settle (the Land)."

The *mitzvah* of *lasheves* is an on-going *mitzvah*,[10] meaning, it is a *mitzvah* to bring children into the world even after one has fulfilled the *mitzvah* of *pru urvu*. The *mitzvah* of *lasheves* also applies to women.[11]

The second of these *mitzvos* is referred to as *la'erev*, "the evening." In *Megillah*

---

4   *Yevamos* 61b.

5   *Shu't Chasam Sofer Even HaEzer* 1:20 (end of responsum).

6   *Shu't Chasam Sofer Even HaEzer* 1:20. See also *Shu't Tzitz Eliezer* 9:51, pg. 222.

7   *Tosafos, Pesachim* 88b and *Bava Basra* 13a s.v. *Kofin*; although these *mitzvos* are technically rabbinic, they are usually treated as much stricter than other rabbinic *mitzvos* since their source is scriptural.

8   *Yeshayahu* 45:18.

9   As heard from Rav Yitzchak Berkovits.

10   See *Igros Moshe Even HaEzer* 4:73, where Rav Moshe Feinstein implies that the *mitzvah* of *lasheves* obligates one to have as many children as possible.

11   *Tosafos, Gittin* 41b s.v. lo; *Tosafos Pesachim* 88b s.v. *Kofin*. (See also *Beis Shmuel Even HaEzer* 1:2.) The *Shu't Chasam Sofer* implies that the requirement of *lasheves* is fulfilled with one child. *Pru urvu* requires a son and a daughter. However, Rav Moshe Feinstein (*Igros Moshe Even HaEzer* 4:73) implies that because of *lasheves*, one is obligated to have as many children as possible. This may not be a contradiction. Rav Moshe may mean that a man's *mitzvah* of *lasheves* requires him to have as many children as possible, whereas *Shu't Chasam Sofer* is referring to the woman's *mitzvah*. Alternatively, *Shu't Chasam Sofer* may be describing a minimum fulfillment, whereas Rav Moshe is saying that the *mitzvah* always continues.

Koheles,[12] it is written, "In the morning sow your seed, and in the evening do not stay your hand, for you know not which will prosper, this or that, or perhaps both will be equally good." The *Gemara*[13] explains this verse means that even if a man had children in his youth, he should continue to have children in his old age.[14]

A woman is not technically required in the *mitzvah* of *la'erev*,[15] however, since a man may not marry more than one wife,[16] a woman may not practice birth control without the consent of her husband.[17]

Foregoing the Positive Commandments of Having Children

Most *halachic* authorities rule that if having a baby in any way physically or emotionally would endanger a woman's life, she is not only allowed to use birth

---

12   *Koheles* 11:6.

13   *Yevamos* 62b.

14   *Even HaEzer* 1:8 rules that when a man remarries he should marry a woman young enough to have children, with the exceptions of (a) certain financial considerations, (b) if he feels that adding new children to his family will create friction between his new wife and the children he has already (Rama ad loc) or (c) if he knows that he can no longer father children (Rama ad loc). Some *halachic* authorities also rule that if he may not be able to keep a younger woman physically satisfied, he should not marry a young woman. (See *Yevamos* 106b, where *yibum* is discouraged in the case of an older man with a younger woman. This *halachah* is quoted in *Even HaEzer* 166:1.)

15   *Tosafos*, *Gittin* 41b.

16   The *Torah* does not prohibit a man from having more than one wife. However, over 1,000 years ago, *Ashkenazi* Jewry accepted that a man not marry more than one woman. This is often referred to as the "*Cherem* of Rabbeinu Gershom," after the great *Torah* leader who promulgated it. (*Cherem* refers to the banishment that was imposed upon a man for violating this decree.) In recent years, *Sefardi* Jewry has, for the most part, accepted this practice as well.

17   The *Shu't Chasam Sofer Yoreh Deah* 172 rules that since the husband cannot marry another wife, he has the right to tell his wife that he wants more children (or a divorce so that he can have more children), even if he already has children and has fulfilled the *mitzvah* of *pru urvu*. Based on the *Shu't Chasam Sofer*, *Pischei Teshuvah* (*Even HaEzer* 23:2) rules that a woman may not practice birth control even when permitted without her husband's permission.

control but is obligated. This *halachic* ruling applies even if the risk to life is remote.[18] This is because the commandment of *pikuach nefesh*, preserving life, is paramount.

Most *halachic* authorities also rule that the use of birth control is allowed in cases where having a child (or another child) would seriously harm a woman's (or her family's) well being.[19]

As we discussed, every decision to forego these paramount *mitzvos* of bringing children into the world may only be made on an individual basis after consultation with a *halachic* authority.

Negative Commandments

In cases where the use of birth control is *halachically* sanctioned, a couple must still not violate any of the negative *mitzvos* associated with preventing pregnancy.

Our first discussion centers around the prohibition of *hotzaas zera levatalah*, wasting seed. This prohibition is derived from the narrative of Tamar in the book of *Bereishis* (Genesis). Here, the *Torah* describes the marriage of Tamar and her second husband, Onan, in which Onan spilled his seed in order to prevent fathering a child with her.

> *Yehudah took a wife for Er, his firstborn, whose name was Tamar. Er, Yehudah's firstborn, was evil in the eyes of* Hashem, *and* Hashem *caused him to die. Then Yehudah said to Onan, "Consort with your brother's wife and enter into a levirate marriage with her and establish offspring for your brother." But Onan knew*

---

[18] *Yevamos* 12b; *Kesubos* 39. However, according to Rabbeinu Tam's approach there is no evidence from these *sugyos* to permit contraception. Thus, there are *halachic* authorities who prohibit birth control, because they rule that *hotzaas zera levatalah* (wasting seed) is a potentially more serious prohibition and consider divorce a better option. (See *Pischei Teshuvah Even HaEzer* 23:2.)

[19] *Yevamos* 65b; quoted in *Even HaEzer* 5:12 and *Beis Shmuel* ad loc. However, some authorities say that this *halachah* no longer applies because of the *cherem* Rabbeinu Gershom (the prohibition of a man taking more than one wife) and rule that birth control is now only allowed in situations of *pikuach nefashos*.

that the seed would not be his;[20] *so it was, that whenever he would consort with his brother's wife, he would let it go to waste on the ground so as not to provide offspring for his brother. What he did was evil in the eyes of* Hashem, *and He caused him (Onan) to die also.*[21]

From the *Torah*, it is clear that if, in the process of having relations, the man spills his seed outside of his wife in order to prevent conception, he has sinned. In addition, any form of intimate relations which spills seed outside the woman's body is forbidden.[22]

We find a discussion of these concepts, as well as the parameters for the different kinds of birth control, in the *Gemara* which discusses three situations where the *Gemara* says it is dangerous for a woman to get pregnant.[23] The first opinion, that of Rabbi Meir, rules that a woman in any of these situations uses[24] a *moch* (literally, cloth) during or after marital relations.

A *moch* most likely meant placing a cloth or absorbent material in the vaginal canal to absorb the seed and thus prevent conception. The three situations listed are:

◆ A girl under the age of 12 (because pregnancy is considered dangerous for a girl this young);

◆ A woman who is pregnant already (because it would be

---

20 *Bereishis* 38:8. Ramban implies that Onan knew, on a mystical level, that the soul of his brother would be reincarnated into the child of such a union and did not want to raise a child that he didn't consider his own. Sforno comments that Onan did not want to share the *mitzvah* of having children with his brother (since the reason he was marrying Tamar was because of her prior marriage to his brother, Er).

21 *Bereishis* 38:6–10; Rashi explains that the use of the word "also" implies that Er died for a similar sin. Radak 38:7 concludes the same through the phrase, "evil in the eyes of *Hashem*," meaning in matters revealed only to *Hashem*, that is, in marital relations, where Er spilled his seed so that Tamar would not conceive (and thus her beauty would not be "marred" by pregnancy).

22 Rama, *Even HaEzer* 25:2.

23 *Yevamos* 12b.

24 According to Rashi and Rabbeinu Tam ad loc., "should use."

dangerous for the fetus if a second, concurrent pregnancy would occur); and

- ◆ A woman who is nursing a baby (because if she were to become pregnant, the first baby would have to be weaned prematurely).

The opposing opinion, that of the Sages, disagrees with the above position and states that in these three situations, relations take place as usual and mercy will come from Heaven (as will be explained below).

Halachah follows the opinion of the Sages. This is because most authorities feel that the dispute between Rabbi Meir and the Sages is *only* concerning these three cases, which are all normal, routine life situations. Thus, the Sages are contending that *Hashem* does not place someone in danger in normal, routine life situations. However, in an unusual situation, such as a case where it is clearly dangerous for a woman to get pregnant, most authorities say that the Sages would rule differently (and allow the use of a *moch*).

In addition, as we will see in our discussion below, many of our contemporary methods of birth control (the pill, spermicides, the IUD and, according to some authorities, the diaphragm) do not share the *halachic* issues that the *moch* does, since they do not involve questions of wasting seed.

Methods of Birth Control

To understand why certain methods of birth control are acceptable in *halachah* and others are not, we must first understand how the above *moch* was used, and how it is viewed in light of the prohibition of wasting seed.

Here, we find two opinions among the early commentaries. One opinion states that the *moch* was inserted *before* marital relations. They maintain that since the woman is not allowed to become pregnant, having relations while a *moch* is inserted is the normal way *for her* to have relations.[25] Thus the seed is not wasted, as

---

[25] Ramban and Ritva, *Kesubos* 39a.

in the case of any woman whose husband is obligated to fulfill the *mitzvah* of *onah* even when she cannot become pregnant — for example, a woman who is sterile, already pregnant or post menopausal.[26]

Others disagree and contend that the *moch* was inserted *after* relations to wipe the area clean.[27] This opinion contends that it is forbidden to have relations with an inserted *moch* because of the prohibition of wasting seed.[28] According to many *halachic* authorities, this opinion contends that it is not permitted to use birth control methods that block seed (for example, a barrier, such as the diaphragm), as these methods are *halachically* equivalent to a *moch*. (Once relations have taken place in a normal way, the subsequent destruction of the seed by wiping the area clean with a *moch* does not violate the prohibition.)

Most authorities agree, however, that in the case of a true danger, if no other options exist for a particular woman, the use of a *moch* during relations is permitted.[29]

We will now examine the various forms of birth control available today and the *halachos* regarding each methods.

Birth Control Pills and Other Hormonal Methods

Birth control pills and other hormonal methods of birth control introduce hormonal changes into the body that prevent pregnancy in three ways, depending on the type of method used:

1. By preventing ovulation (the release of an egg by the ovary),
2. By creating a hostile environment in the uterus for implantation of an embryo (a fertilized egg) into the uterine wall, and

---

[26] *Igros Moshe Even HaEzer* 1:63. Rav Moshe Feinstein rules that the *mitzvah* of *onah* makes the *zera* not *levatalah*, just as relations during pregnancy and after menopause do not cause *zera levatalah*.

[27] Rabbeinu Tam, quoted in *Tosafos, Kesubos* 39a.

[28] *Shu't Chasam Sofer Yoreh Deah* 172.

[29] *Igros Moshe Even HaEzer* 1:63. Rav Moshe Feinstein rules that the *mitzvah* of *onah* makes the *zera* not *levatalah* just as relations during pregnancy and after menopause are not considered *zera levatalah*.

3. By causing a buildup of cervical mucous, making it difficult for the seed to reach the egg.

In a situation when birth control is warranted, many *halachic* authorities allow the use of birth control pills and other hormonal methods. Since marital relations take place in the normal way, there is no issue of a *moch*, and seed is not considered wasted.

However, some *halachic* authorities prohibit or discourage their usage for two reasons:

1. Concerns about *niddah*, since many women experience break-through bleeding with these methods[30] and

2. Concerns about the potentially severe side effects on the woman's health, both in the short term and in the long term.[31]

(Because of these side effects, it should be noted that for many women, hormonal methods of birth control are not a good option.)

Intrauterine Device — IUD

The IUD, or Intrauterine Device, is a small device which is inserted into the uterus by a doctor. Exactly how an IUD prevents pregnancy is not known. In

---

[30]   *Igros Moshe Even HaEzer* 2:17 rules that a woman should preferably not use the pill because of *niddah* (spotting) problems. Here, Rav Moshe Feinstein says that if she does use the pill, she must leave a *moch* in the entire first month to see that she does not bleed because of the pill. If she sees no blood the first month, she may proceed to use the pill without this precaution. In *Even HaEzer* 3:24, he adds that if she cannot keep a *moch* in the entire month, then it is sufficient instead to wear white undergarments the entire month, but they must be tight-fitting. In addition, she must do at least one *bedikah* a day, always use a white pad and must check the water when she urinates. In *Even HaEzer* 4:67, 69, he reiterates that he does not think using the pill is a solution for a woman for whom it is dangerous to become pregnant and instead recommends the diaphragm.

[31]   In *Igros Moshe Even HaEzer* 4:72, Rav Moshe Feinstein says that the pill is not good for a woman's health. In his response, Rav Moshe adds that the person asking the question should point this out to the doctor, who is apparently unaware of this problem. *Igros Moshe Even HaEzer* 4:74:2 also mentions health concerns about the pill. In *Even HaEzer* 4:67, 69, Rav Moshe says that he does not think using the pill is a solution for a woman for whom it is dangerous to become pregnant and instead recommends the diaphragm.

some IUD's, it is assumed that the device acts as a spermicide, blocking and debilitating sperm. Another theory is that the device doesn't allow the implantation of a fertilized egg into the uterine wall, possibly due to creating an inflammation in the uterine wall, causing a spontaneous abortion in cases where conception has taken place.

Many *halachic* authorities allow the usage of an IUD. Some allow its usage but with reservations.[32] Yet other authorities are opposed to the IUD because of the concern about an early stage abortion.[33] Others forbid it because of health dangers involved.[34] Still others forbid its use because of the problem of irregular bleeding while keeping the laws of *niddah*.[35]

Spermicides

Spermicides are chemically prepared creams, foams, jellies and suppositories which work by destroying the sperm, thus preventing it from reaching an egg. The majority of *halachic* authorities rule that using a spermicide is not considered wasting seed, since relations with a spermicide are still considered a normal act of relations.[36] However, a minority of authorities rule that the use of a spermicide violates the prohibition of wasting seed.[37]

---

[32] *Shu't Minchas Yitzchak* 6:87 rules that one should be concerned because of spotting and permits its usage only in *pikuach nefashos* situations.

[33] *Shu't Tzitz Eliezer* 9:51:2:3:7 rules that it is better to use a diaphragm than an IUD, possibly because of concerns that IUD might be considered an early stage abortion. He maintains that an IUD involves a more severe case of *hotzaas zera levatalah* than a diaphragm, because the *zera* may be fertilized.

[34] Potentially dangerous side effects of IUD's include tubal infections and pelvic inflammatory disease (PID), which can lead to permanent sterility.

[35] *Igros Moshe Even HaEzer* 3:21 and 4:68. In addition to bleeding between periods, IUD's can cause heavier and longer periods, with more cramping.

[36] Rav Moshe Feinstein (*Igros Moshe Even HaEzer* 1:62) rules that spermicides are permitted even when not a case of *pikuach nefashos*. He compares it to *kos shel ikrin* (the root that sterilized, see *Shabbos* 111a), since there is no physical block. Rav Moshe rules that the fact that it destroys the *zera* is not considered *hotzaas zera levatalah* because the relations take place normally.

[37] *Shu't Tzitz Eliezer* 9:51:2:3:5 rules that since a spermacide destroys the *zera*, it is an act of *hotzaas zera levatalah* and worse than using a *moch*.

Many spermicides have a high failure rate and, thus, are not adequate protection against pregnancy in cases that are life threatening or where a woman needs maximum protection. However, they can be used in conjunction with other methods of birth control[38] to increase their efficiency.

Spermicides are not associated with dangerous side effects.[39]

Diaphragm

A diaphragm is a soft latex cup that is filled with spermicide and inserted internally before relations. The diaphragm works in two ways: As a barrier to the cervical opening and as a means to make the spermicide more effective.

Many *halachic* authorities rule that using a diaphragm falls under the category of having relations while wearing a *moch* (a barrier) and thus oppose its usage. Others allow its usage but only in *pikuach nefesh* situations.[40] Still others rule that the diaphragm is placed high enough in the vaginal canal that it does not qualify as a *moch*.[41]

The effectiveness of a diaphragm depends on using it correctly. This means it must be fitted properly, checked annually and refitted after every pregnancy or a weight gain or loss of five to ten pounds. It must also be left in place for six hours after relations[42] (and additional spermicide must be applied if relations are repeated within that time).

---

[38] For example, abstention during the fertile days or while nursing a baby (for a woman whose period has not resumed after childbirth). Note that abstention during the fertile days still requires that the couple ask a question to their *halachic* authoritiy.

[39] However, some women (and men) experience minor skin irritation from these preparations.

[40] Rav Moshe Feinstein considers the diaphragm a *moch* (*Igros Moshe Even HaEzer* 4:69) but allows its usage in *pikuach nefashos* situations (*Even HaEzer* 1:63), reasoning that for a woman who may not become pregnant, marital relations with a *moch* are considered normal relations and not *hotzaas zera levatalah* (since the husband still has a *mitzvah* of *onah*).

[41] *Shu't Maharsham* 1:58. This was also the opinion of Rav Shlomo Zalman Auerbach (see *Nishmas Avraham* Vol. 3 pg. 63).

[42] Although side effects of the diaphragm are not common and usually minor (e.g., skin sensitivity to the spermicide), if a diaphragm is left in place too long, the possibility of toxic shock syndrome exists.

Condom

A condom is a thin shield made out of latex rubber, polyurethane or animal tissue and is (usually) worn by the man. The condom works by trapping the seed, thereby preventing it from entering the woman's body. It is generally assumed that a condom is not an acceptable form of contraception, however, in a case where conception would be *pikuach nefashos* and no other method is possible, a couple should consult their *halachic* authority regarding the use of this method.[43]

Abstention

The *Torah* directs a husband to give his wife conjugal pleasure;[44] this is his obligation and her right. A woman for whom pregnancy would be harmful does not have to give up this right (by abstaining from marital relations).[45]

Partial abstention (during the most fertile days) avoids many of the *halachic* and health-related problems associated with the various methods of birth control discussed above. However, partial absention can be fraught with failure, depending on the circumstances, and is therefore not appropriate in situations involving *pikuach nefashos*. In addition, it is not required by *halachah* that a couple even partially forego marital relations.[46]

---

[43]   *Shu't Achiezer* 3:24:5. *Igros Moshe Even HaEzer* 1:67.
[44]   *Shemos* 21:10.
[45]   *Kesubos* 61b, 62a.
[46]   *Kesubos* 61b, 62a.

Glossary

adam l'chaveiro — between man and his fellowman.

al netilas yadayim — a blessing recited upon washing one's hands.

al titosh toras imecha — "Do not forsake the teaching of your mother" from *Mishlei* (Proverbs) 1:8.

amidah — the main prayer of each prayer service; also called the *shemonah esrei*. It is recited standing (*omed*, in Hebrew), hence its name, the *amidah*.

Amora/Amorayim (plural) — rabbinic scholars of the period of the *Gemara*, who lived approximately between the years of 200—400 CE.

aneinu (*prayer*) — a prayer recited during the *amidah* on fast days.

Anshei Kenesses HaGedolah — literally, the Men of the Great Assembly. The 120 great *Torah* leaders who lived at the time of the building of the Second Temple, c.350 years BCE.

arayos — severe sexual prohibitions.

ayna kavua — non-established. In the context of the laws of *niddah*, a period that has not repeated its pattern three times in a row.

b'simcha — with happiness.

bedikah/bedikos (plural) — a check. In the context of the laws of *niddah*, an internal check of the vaginal area done with a small, white cloth.

beinonis — average, mean.

Beis HaMikdash — our Holy Temple in Jerusalem.

besulah — a virgin.

besulim — the hymen.

Biurim — explanations, commentary.

bodkos — *niddah* nurses. Women who are specially trained to check the source of a woman's bleeding.

bris milah — ritual circumcision.

chafifah — literally, scrubbing. A term used to describe the preparations done prior to immersing in the *mikveh* — specifically, bathing and washing and combing the hair.

challah — the consecrated portion separated from bread dough.

chassidim — In common use, those who follow the teachings of Rav Yisroel Baal Shem Tov and his disciples.

chatzitzah — an intervening substance.

chazakah — in our context, one's personal status quo.

cherem of Rabbeinu Gershom — in our context, the prohibition of a man having more than one wife.

chodesh — month.

choson — groom.

chumrah — a *halachic* stringency.

chupah — the wedding canopy; also refers to the wedding ceremony.

chupas niddah — a situation in which the bride is *niddah* at her wedding ceremony.

churban — destruction; usually refers to the destruction of our Holy Temple in Jerusalem.

dam besulim — bleeding caused by the tearing of the hymen.

dam makeh — bleeding caused by a wound or trauma.

davening — praying or prayer.

dibuk — a "wandering soul" that can possess the body of a human being.

ervah — someone with whom having intimate relations involves a severe prohibition.

Gan Eden — the Garden of Eden; paradise.

gezeirah — a rabbinic decree.

gris — a measurement, which is about 19 millimeters in diameter or slightly larger than a U.S. dime or an Israeli one shekel coin.

guf — body.

haflagah/haflagah onah — the segment of time when a woman anticipates the onset of her period based on the number of days that intervened between her last two periods.

halachah/ halachos (plural) — Jewish law.

harchakos — literally, "distancings." The *halachos* that govern the interactions between a couple when the wife is *niddah*.

hargashah — a sensation of the cervix opening.

Hashem — God.

hataras nedarim — annulling vows.

hefsek taharah — internal check that verifies one's period has ended.

hotzaas zera levatalah — spilling (wasting) of seed.

iyun — checking over; specifically, the final check required by *halachah* before immersing in the *mikveh*.

Kabbalah (noun)/ *kabbalistic* (adjective) — the mystical side of Jewish teaching.

kallah — bride.

karais — a serious punishment of the *Torah*.

kavua — established. In our context, a period cycle that has repeated itself three times in a row.

kedushah — holiness; sanctity.

kesem — a stain. In our context, refers to a possible blood stain found after no sensation of a flow.

kiddush — the ceremony performed at the beginning of *Shabbos* and *Yom Tov* evening and morning.

kodoshim — sacred items that derive their holiness from their relationship to the Holy Temple.

kohen — men who descend patrilineally from Aharon, Moshe's brother, and who still have the sanctity with which he was endowed.

kol ishah — a woman's singing voice.

kos shel ikrin — an herbal potion that was used in *Talmudic* times for a woman to render herself sterile.

la'erev — the *mitzvah* to continue to have children after one already has a son and a daughter.

lasheves — to exist, settle or sit; refers to God's desire that the world should be populated.

levatalah — in vain.

meinekes — a nursing mother; also refers to any woman during the first 24 months after childbirth.

mekabel tumah — an item that is capable of becoming *tamei* (ritually impure).

melachos — forbidden work activities of *Shabbos* and *Yom Tov*.

mesorah — the Jewish tradition.

mezeigas ha-cos — pouring of a cup.

middos — literally, measurements. Refers also to character traits.

miderabbanan — a rabbinically introduced prohibition or requirement.

mikveh/mikvaos (plural) — ritual bath.

mil — a measure of distance of 2000 *amos* (approximately one kilometer). Used extensively by our Sages to measure time, as in the amount of time it takes to walk a *mil*.

minchah katanah — a point of time in the day which is one half hour after 3/4 of the daytime hours have passed (determined by measuring the amount of time between sunrise and sunset).

minhag/minhagim (plural) — custom.

minhag Yisrael — an established Jewish practice.

mitzvah/mitzvos (plural) — commandment.

mitzvah rabbah — an important (literally, big) commandment.

moch — a piece of cotton or other soft cloth.

moch dachuk — a piece of cotton or other soft cloth that is put into the vaginal canal to determine that all *niddah* bleeding has ceased; used between sundown and nightfall after making the *hefsek taharah*.

motzaei (as in *motzaei Shabbos* or *motzaei Yom Tov*) — the night after.

nazir — a person who takes a vow that prohibits him or her from drinking wine or consuming other grape products and coming in contact with a dead person.

negiyah — touching.

niddah — literally, separate. Used to refer to a woman who may not have physical contact with her husband; also used to refer to the status of such a woman.

Ohr Zarua onah — the day or night before another *onah* when a couple may not be together in anticipation of the wife's period.

onah — (1) a measurement of time; half a day. The daytime *onah* is from sunrise to sunset, and the nighttime *onah* is from sunset to sunrise. (2) The *mitzvah* of *onah* refers to a husband's *Torah* obligation to please his wife and be intimate with her physically and emotionally.

onah beinonis — the segment of time when a woman anticipates the onset of her period; calculated by counting 30 days from her last period.

onos — plural of *onah*.

pesichas hakever — opening of the uterus.

pidyon haben — redemption of the firstborn.

pikuach nefesh — life threatening.

pirsah niddah — became *niddah*. In our context, refers to a *kallah* who became *niddah* after the *chupah*, but before the couple experienced marital relations.

posek/poskim (plural) — *halachic* authority.

pru urvu — the *mitzvah* of procreation.

rebbetzin — a rabbi's wife; used also to refer to a Jewishly well-educated woman or teacher.

rishon/rishonim (plural) — rabbinic authorities who lived between the 11th and 14th centuries. The basis of most of our observance of *halachah* comes from the interpretations of the *rishonim*.

rosh chodesh — first day of the Jewish month.

ruach ra — an evil spirit.

savta — grandmother.

seudas mitzvah — a meal eaten on the occasion of the performing of a *mitzvah*, for example, after a *bris*.

Shabbos — the Jewish Sabbath.

shalom bayis — peace in the home. Used to refer to a good relationship between husband and wife.

Shechinah — the Divine presence.

sheid — a demon.

Shema — central Jewish prayer, beginning with the sentence *Shema Yisrael, Adonoy Eloheinu, Adonoy echad*.

Sheva Brachos — literally, seven blessings. Used to refer to the festive meals eaten to celebrate a newly married couple (the seven blessings that are said under the *chupah* are also recited at these meals).

shivah — literally, seven. Used to refer to the Jewish seven-day mourning period.

shivah nekiyim — the "Seven Clean Days" that a woman observes prior to immersing in the *mikveh*.

shu't — an abbreviation for *shaylos u'teshuvos* (questions and answers); responsa collection or a specific responsum.

siyum — a festive meal celebrating the completion of a *Torah* learning project.

sugyah/sugyos (plural) — a *halachic* subject.

ta'anis — a fast day.

ta'aniyos tzadikim — a fast day that is observed only by the particularly righteous.

tachanun — a special prayer recited on weekdays immediately after the *amidah*.

taharah — ritual purity.

tahor — ritually pure.

takanah — an injunction or improvement.

takanas chachomim — a rabbinic injunction.

talis katan — a (relatively) small, four-cornered garment that contains *tzitzis* on its corners.

tamei — ritually impure.

tanna — sages whose teachings about our Oral Law were written down in the *Mishnah*.

tefach — a measurement about the size of a fist.

tefilin — phylacteries.

temei'ah — ritually impure.

terumah — the sanctified portion of produce.

tevilah — immersion.

tikun olam — repairing the world.

tikun — a repair.

tumah — ritual impurity.

tzadikim — righteous individuals.

tzeis/tzeis hakochavim — literally, when the stars come out; *halachic* nightfall.

tzelem Elohim — the image of God.

vesasos — times when a woman is anticipating her period.

veses — singular of *vesasos*.

veses hachodesh — the *veses* that is caused by the date a woman's period arrived the previous Hebrew month.

veses haflagah — the *veses* that is caused by the number of days that intervened between a woman's last two periods.

veses haflagah kavua — an established interval *veses*; a period cycle based on the repeating of the same number of days intervening between a woman's periods.

veses haguf — anticipation of a period because of specific physical symptoms.

veses hashavua — anticipation of a period based on the day of the week.

veses kavua — an established *veses*.

veses she'ayna kavua — a non-established *veses*.

Vidui — confession.

yeshivah/yeshivos (plural) — place or school of higher education for the study of *Torah*.

yetzer harah — the evil inclination.

yichud — seclusion; usually refers to the prohibition of a man and a woman being secluded together.

yoledes — a woman in, or shortly after, childbirth.

yom hachodesh — the date of the month.

Yom Tov — holiday from the *Torah*.

zatz'l — abbreviation for "May the memory of this righteous person be for a blessing."

zavah — a type of uterine bleeding occurring at a time when a woman is not expecting her period.

zavah gadolah — a woman who had three consecutive days of uterine bleeding when she was not expecting her period.

zavah katanah — a woman who had less than three consecutive days of uterine bleeding when she was not expecting her period.

zekainah — a post-menopausal woman who is also elderly.

zera — semen; seed.

Sources

Achai Gaon, Rav c. 680–752, known as The Gaon, or head of the *Yeshivah* Academy of Pumbedisa, Babylonia; authored one of the earliest post-*Talmudic* extant works, entitled the *She'iltos*.

Aishel Avraham Work authored by Rav Avraham David Vohrman, 1771–1840, who is usually referred to as the Butchacher Rav for the position he held for 26 years. This work is often colloquially referred to as *Aishel Avraham of Butchach* to avoid confusion with an earlier work, the *Aishel Avraham* section of the *Pri Megadim*, which is a supercommentary on the *Magen Avraham* on *Orach Chayim*, written by Rav Yosef Teumim Frankel.

Ari Rav Yitzchak Luria, 1534–1572, possibly the most famous *kabbalist* of the last thousand years, who lived his last years in Tzefas (Safed). The name Ari, which means "lion," was probably originally an acronym for *Ashkenazi* Rav Yitzchak, since he was an *Ashkenazi* resident of an almost exclusively *Sefardi* community.

Aruch HaShulchan *Halachah* work by Rav Yechiel Michel Epstein, 1829–1902, rav of Novardok, Russia (now Novogrudok, Belarus); considered one of the final *halachic* authorities of his generation.

Atzei Levonah 19th century commentary on *Shulchan Aruch* by Rav Nisan Aaronson.

Auerbach, Rav Shlomo Zalman 1910–1995, of Jerusalem. One of the greatest *halachic* authorities of our time.

Avodah Zarah Tractate of the *Talmud* whose primary subject is idol worship and the *halachos* dealing with Jewish/non-Jewish relations.

Baalei HaNefesh *Halachah* work on the laws of *niddah* by Rabbi Avraham ben David of Posquieres, Provence, France, c.1120 – c.1197, the Raavad. (Note: There are several early *Torah* scholars who are called Raavad, all as acronyms of their names.)

Ba'er Heiteiv An early anthologized commentary on *Shulchan Aruch* that was later modified by different editors in different editions. The section on *Yoreh Deah* is usually accredited to Rav Zecharyah Mendel, the rav of Belz, Ukraine.

Bach Commentary on the *Tur Shulchan Aruch* written by Rav Yoel Sirkis of Poland, 1561–1640.

Badei HaShulchan Multi-volume contemporary commentary on *Shulchan Aruch Yoreh Deah* authored by Rav Feivel Cohen of Brooklyn, NY.

Bamidbar The biblical book of *Numbers*.

Bava Basra Tractate of the *Talmud* that discusses the subjects of relations between neighbors, purchases, inheritance and wills.

Bava Kama Tractate of the *Talmud* that discusses the subject of damages.

Bedek HaBayis Corrections and additions of Rav Yosef Caro, 1488–1575, to his own commentary on the *Tur* (called the *Beis Yosef*). It is published now as part of the *Beis Yosef*.

Beis Meir Commentary on *Shulchan Aruch* by Rav Meir Posner, the rav of Shutland, Germany in the early 19th century.

Beis Shmuel One of the major commentaries on *Shulchan Aruch Even HaEzer* authored by Rav Shmuel ben Uri Shraga Feivush of Poland, c. 1640 – c. 1700.

Beis Yosef Written by Rav Yosef Caro, 1488–1575. *Beis Yosef* is a commentary on the *Tur Shulchan Aruch*, which was written by Rav Yaakov, son of the Rosh (Rabbeinu Asher). Rav Yosef Caro wrote this work prior to his writing of the *Shulchan Aruch*.

Bereishis The biblical book of *Genesis*.

Bereishis Rabbah An anthology of *Midrashim* on the biblical book of *Bereishis*.

Berkovits, Rav Yitzchak A prominent international *posek* and educator; founder and head of *The Jerusalem Kollel*, whose purpose is to train *yeshivah* students of the highest caliber to assume positions of leadership and outreach in Jewish communities worldwide. As the former *menahel ruchani* of *Aish HaTorah Yeshivah* for over sixteen years, Rav Berkovits developed and taught the *Aish HaTorah Smichah Program*, guiding over 100 students through the successful completion of many areas of *halachah* and practical rabbinics.

Birkei Yosef Commentary on *Shulchan Aruch* by Rav Chayim Yosef David Azulai, 1724–1807, usually referred to by his acronym, the Chida. The Chida was born in Israel but traveled in Europe extensively as a fundraiser for Jewish communities; he also authored dozens of works on *halachah*, *Kabbalah* and other Jewish subjects.

Bi'ur Halachah Analytic commentary on *Orach Chayim*, authored by Rav Yisroel Meir HaKohen, the famed *Chofetz Chayim*, 1838–1933; printed side-by-side with his *halachic* conclusions, the *Mishnah Berurah*.

Brachos Tractate of the *Talmud* that discusses prayers and blessings.

Chavos Daas Commentary on *Shulchan Aruch* authored by Rav Yaakov Loeberbaum of Poland and Germany, 1760–1832; often referred to in *halachic* literature either as Rav Yaakov of Lisa, or by his works, *Nesivos HaMishpat* or *Chavos Daas*.

Chayei Adam *Halachic* compendium on the subjects of *Orach Chayim* authored by Rav Avraham Danzig, 1748–1820, early 19th century *halachic* authority of Vilna, Poland/Russia (now Vilnius, Lithuania). Until the publishing of the *Mishnah Berurah*, this work was often treated as the final *halachic* conclusion.

Chazon Ish Seven-volume *halachah* work by Rav Avraham Yeshayah Karelitz, of Polish Lithuania and Bnei Brak, 1878–1953, covering the length and breadth of *halachah*.

Chelkas Mechokek Major commentary on *Shulchan Aruch Even HaEzer* authored in the 17th century by Rav Moshe Lima.

Chochmas Adam *Halachah* work on the subjects of *Yoreh Deah* authored by Rav Avraham Danzig, 1748–1820, early 19th century *halachic* authority of Vilna, Poland/Russia (now Vilnius, Lithuania).

Chullin Tractate of the *Talmud* that discusses the subject of kosher meat.

Chut Shani Contemporary *halachah* work on the laws of *niddah* based on lectures delivered by Rav Nissim Karelitz of Bnei Brak.

Dagul Mei'Revavah Commentary on *Shulchan Aruch* authored by Rav Yechezkel Landau of Prague, 1713–1793.

Darchei Chachmah Contemporary commentary on the *Chochmas Adam*, authored by Rav Betzalel Gincharski of Tifrach, Israel.

Darchei Moshe Commentary on the *Tur Shulchan Aruch* authored by Rama, Rav Moshe Isserles, which he used as a basis for his glosses to the *Shulchan Aruch*.

Darchei Teshuvah Anthology of responsa and late commentaries on the *Shulchan Aruch Yoreh Deah* published between the 1890's and the 1930's; authored by Rav Tzvi Hirsh Shapiro of Munkacs, Hungary (now Mukachevo, Ukraine) and completed by his son and successor, Rav Chaim Elazar Shapiro.

Devarim The biblical book of *Deuteronomy*.

Dvar Halachah A late 20th century *halachah* work on the laws of *yichud* by Rav Avraham HaLevi Horowitz.

Eider, Rav Shimon A contemporary *halachic* authority of Lakewood, NJ; author of *Halachos of Niddah*.

Eiger, Rav Akiva 1762–1838. The *halachic* authority of his generation who served as rav of several communities in Germany and Poland.

Eliyahu Rabbah An early commentary on the *Shulchan Aruch* and *Levush, Orach Chayim* authored by Rav Eliyahu Shapiro of Prague, c.1660–1712.

Eruvin Tractate of the *Talmud* that discusses carrying on *Shabbos* and the laws of *eruv*.

Even HaEzer Section of *Tur* or *Shulchan Aruch* that discusses the laws governing relationships between men and women.

Feinstein, Rav Moshe 1895–1986, of Russia and the United States; considered the greatest *halachic* authority of our time.

Forst, Rav Binyomin A contemporary *halachic* authority of Far Rockaway, New York; author of several *halachah* works on the laws of *brachos* and *niddah*.

Gemara The authoritative earliest commentary on the *Mishnah*, which, together with the *Mishnah*, comprises the basis of the *Oral Torah*. The *Gemara* is the recording of the discussions of the *yeshivos* in Babylonia and Israel that took place roughly 1,700—1,800 years ago.

Gilyon Maharsha Notes on *Shulchan Aruch* by Rav Shlomo Eiger, 1786–1852, who succeeded his father Rav Akiva Eiger as rav of Posen.

Gittin Tractate of the *Talmud* that discusses the laws of divorce.

HaEmek Davar Commentary on the *Torah* authored by Rav Naftali Tzvi Yehudah Berlin, 1817–1893, usually called by his acronym, Netziv; the *Rosh Yeshivah* of the *Yeshivah* of Volozhin, Belarus.

Heller, Rebbetzin Tzipporah A well-known international educator, author and *Torah* scholar; since 1980, Rebbetzin Heller has been a full-time faculty member of *Neve Yerushalayim* in Jerusalem, where her areas of expertise include textual analysis of Biblical literature and Jewish philosophy.

Henkin, Rav Yosef Eliyahu 1880–1973, of Russia and the United States; considered one of the greatest *halachic* authorities of his generation.

Hilchos Issurei Bi'ah Section of the Rambam's *Mishneh Torah* that discusses the laws of forbidden sexual relationships.

Hilchos Niddah The laws of *niddah* either in the *Tur, Shulchan Aruch* or other works.

Hilchos Shabbos Section of the Rambam's *Mishneh Torah* or of other *halachah* works that discusses the laws of *Shabbos*.

Hilchos Teshuvah Section of the Rambam's *Mishneh Torah* that discusses the laws of repentance.

Hirsch, Rav Shimshon Raphael 1808–1888, author, scholar and leader of Orthodox Jewry in Germany.

Igeres HaKodesh A work on the holiness of marriage by the Ramban.

Igros Moshe Responsa authored by Rav Moshe Feinstein, 1895–1986, of Russia and the United States, considered the greatest *halachic* authority of his generation. *Igros Moshe* spans all sections of the *Shulchan Aruch* on contemporary issues.

Kaf HaChayim *Halachah* work on *Orach Chayim* and *Yoreh Deah* authored by Rav Yaakov Chayim Sofer of Iraq and Israel, 1870–1939.

Kehilos Yaakov Multi-volume work of essays on the *Gemara* by Rav Yaakov Yisrael Kanievsky, 1899–1985, of Bnei Brak, often called the Steipler Gaon (after the location of the first *yeshivah* in which he studied in Horosteipel, Ukraine).

Keneses Yechezkel Responsa authored by Rav Yechezkel Katzenellenbogen in the 18th century.

Kesubos Tractate of the *Talmud* that discusses the laws governing marriages.

Kiddushin Tractate of the *Talmud* that discusses the laws of weddings.

Kitzur Shulchan Aruch Popular *halachah* compendium authored by Rav Shlomo Ganzfried of Hungary, 1804–1886.

Koheles *Ecclesiastes* in English. One of the books of the *Tanach* authored by Shlomo HaMelech (King Solomon).

Kolbo A *halachah* compendium based on the *Orchos Chayim* of Rav Aharon HaKohen of Lunel, whose authorship is uncertain.

Lechem VeSimlah Commentary on *Hilchos Niddah* by Rav Shlomo Ganzfried of Hungary, 1804–1886.

Machatzis Hashekel Commentary on *Orach Chayim* and *Yoreh Deah* authored by Rav Shmuel HaLevi Kellin of Germany and Poland, 1720–1806.

Machazeh Eliyahu Contemporary *halachah* work by Rav Pesach Eliyahu Falk of Gateshead, England.

Magen Avraham Major commentary on *Shulchan Aruch Orach Chayim* by Rav Avraham Gombiner of Poland, 1634–1682.

Maharam Rottenberg Rav Meir of Rottenberg, Germany. Main *Ashkenazi halachic* authority of the 13th century.

Mahari Abohav Rav Yitzchak Abohav, 1433–1493, a *halachic* authority in Spain who was exiled in the Spanish expulsion. He died in Oporto, Portugal.

Maharil A *halachah* work by Rav Yaakov Moelin, c.1365–1427; includes discussion of prevalent *Torah* practices of the German Jewish (*Ashkenazi*) communities.

Maharshal Rav Shlomo Luria, 1510–1573, one of the major *halachic* authorities of his generation and author of many *halachah* works.

Maharsham Rav Shalom Mordechai Shvadron, often referred to by his last position as the Rav of Bruzhan (Galicia); major *halachic* authority of his generation, the late 19th and early 20th centuries.

Marei Kohen A contemporary work on the laws of *niddah* by Rav Yitzchak Mordechai Rubin of Har Nof, Jerusalem.

Me'il Tzedakah A *halachah* work authored in the 18th century by Rav Eliyahu ben Avraham Shlomo HaKohen.

Melachim *Kings* in English. One of the books of the *Tanach*.

Mesechta Kallah One of the parts of the Oral *Torah* that was not codified into *Mishnah*, but instead into small "tractates;" discusses the *halachos* pertaining to a bride.

Michtav Mei'Eliyahu Books on Jewish thought by Rav Eliyahu Dessler, 1891–1954; written by his disciples based on his notes and lectures.

Midrash The allegorical and ethical teachings of our Sages.

Midrash Rabbah Early anthology of *Midrashim* on the *Torah* and the *megilos*.

Mishlei *Proverbs* in English. One of the books of the *Tanach*.

Mishnah The most basic work of the Oral Law. The *Torah* given to the Jewish people at Mount Sinai was composed of two components: The written *Torah* and its extensive orally transmitted commentary, called the Oral Law. The Oral Law forms the basis of Jewish observance. It was later codified into the *Mishnah* and the *Gemara*. The *Mishnah* is the first redaction of the Oral Law. It was organized and edited by Rabbi Yehudah HaNasi, the head of the Jewish community, around the year 200 C.E.

Mishnah Berurah A commentary on *Shulchan Aruch Orach Chayim* authored by Rav Yisroel Meir HaKohen, the *Chofetz Chayim*; considered by many as the most authoritative commentary in this area of *halachah*.

Mor U'Ketziyah A commentary on *Shulchan Aruch Orach Chayim* by Rav Yaakov Emden of Altoona, Germany, 1698–1776.

Mordechai A *halachah* work that anthologized opinions of earlier *Ashkenazi* authorities written by Rav Mordechai ben Hillel who was martyred in Nuremberg,
Germany in 1298.

Nachalas Shivah A *halachah* work whose primary purpose is to present the correct
form of various *halachic* documents and the reasoning for the author's conclusions; authored by Rav Shmuel ben David HaLevi of Poland and German, 1624–
1681, a disciple of the *Taz.*

Nekudos HaKesef A supercommentary authored by Rav Shabsei HaKohen, the
author of the *Sifsei Cohen* (usually called by its initials, the *Shach*) on *Shulchan
Aruch Yoreh Deah*, in which he refutes opinions of the *Taz.*

Niddah Tractate of the *Talmud* that discusses the laws of marriage and of transac-
tions.

Nimla Tal Contemporary work on the laws of *Shabbos* authored by Rav Yirmiyohu
Kaganoff originally of the United States, now of Jerusalem.

Nishmas Avraham A contemporary anthology of medical-related *halachah* authored
by Dr. Avraham S. Avraham of Jerusalem.

Nisuin KeHilchasah A contemporary anthology on the laws of marriage by Rav
Binyomin Adler of Jerusalem.

Ohalos Tractate of the *Talmud* that discusses the laws of *tumah* spread through roofs
and buildings.

Ohr Zarua A 13th century *halachah* work authored by Rav Yitzchak of Vienna.

Orach Chayim The sections of *Tur* and *Shulchan Aruch* that discuss the laws of prayer,
blessings, *Shabbos, Yom Tov* and other laws that occur in a regular cycle (daily
or annually).

Orchos Chayim An early *halachah* work authored by Rav Aharon HaKohen of Lunel
in the early 14th century.

Path of the Just A classic work of Jewish ethics by Rav Moshe Chaim Luzzatto of
18th century Italy and Israel.

Peah Tractate of the *Talmud* that discusses the laws of charitable gifts.

Peirush Maharzu A commentary on the *Midrash Rabbah* authored by Rav Ze'ev Wolff
Einhorn of Horodna, Poland (now Grodno, Belarus).

Pesachim Tractate of the *Talmud* dealing with the laws of *Pesach.*

Pischei Teshuvah A 19th century anthologized commentary on the *Shulchan Aruch* by Rav Tzvi Hirsch Eizenstadt, the rav of Ottian, Poland, that quotes primarily from responsa.

Piskei Teshuvos A contemporary anthologized commentary on the *Shulchan Aruch Orach Chayim* authored by Rav Simcha Rabinowitz of Jerusalem.

Pleisi A classic commentary of *Shulchan Aruch Yoreh Deah* authored by Rav Yonasan Eibeschutz, 1690–1764, who was the rav of several prominent communities in central Europe.

Posayach Shaar A contemporary *halachah* work on the laws of *niddah* authored by Rav Shalom Friedman of London, a *dayan* (judge) in the *beis din* (court) of the chareidi *Torah* community of London.

Pri Megadim A supercommentary on *Shulchan Aruch*, *Orach Chayim* and *Yoreh Deah* authored by Rav Yosef Teumim Frankel, 1727–1792, of Poland and Germany. This work is technically a commentary on the *Shach*, *Taz* and *Magen Avraham*, the major commentaries on these sections of *Shulchan Aruch*.

Raavad There are several early *halachic* authorities by this name. The Raavad quoted in this book is Rav Avraham ben David of 12th century Posquieres, France (a city in the Provence area), who authored *Baalei HaNefesh*; the author of the first commentary on the Rambam's *Mishneh Torah*.

Rabbeinu Tam Rav Yaakov ben Meir, of Northern France, 1100–1171, who was one of the earliest and probably the most influential of the *Baalei Tosafos*.

Rabbi Eliezer A famed *tanna* often quoted in the *Mishnah*.

Rabbi Meir A famed *tanna* often quoted in the *Mishnah*.

Radak Rav David Kimchi, 1160–1235, of the Provence area of France; Bible commentator and grammarian.

Radbaz Rav David ben Zimra, 1480–1573, who was one of the main *halachic* authorities of his time; served as the chief rabbi of Egypt for over forty years before settling in Israel.

Rama Rav Moshe Isserles of Krakow, Poland, d.1572. Author of glosses to the *Shulchan Aruch* that became the main source of normative *halachah* for *Ashkenazi* Jewry.

Rambam Rav Moshe ben Maimon, or Maimonides, 1135–1204, of Spain, North Africa, and Israel; prolific author of philosophical and religious works; considered one of the greatest (if not the greatest) scholars in Jewish history.

Ramban Rav Moshe ben Nachman, or Nachmanides, 1194–1270, of Spain and Israel; author of numerous works on Jewish thought and *halachah*.

Rashba Rav Shlomo ben Aderes, 1235–1310, of Barcelona, Spain, author of many *halachic* and *Talmudic* works.

Rashi Rav Shlomo Yitzchaki (or Rav Shlomo, the son of Yitzchak), the greatest teacher of the Jewish people in the last thousand years; authored commentaries on *Tanach* and the *Gemara*.

Reishis Chachmah An ethical, *kabbalistic* work by Rav Eliyahu de Vidas of 16th century Israel.

Ritva Rav Yom Tov ben Ashvili, an early 14th century Spanish *halachic* authority and commentator on the *Gemara*.

Rokeach 13th century *halachah* work authored by Rav Elazar Rokeach of Worms, Germany.

Sdei Chemed *Halachah* anthology authored by Rav Chayim Chizkiyah Medini of Jerusalem, the Crimea and Hebron, 1832–1904.

Seder HaYom *Halachic/kabbalistic* guide authored by Rav Moshe Ibn Makir in the 16th century.

Sefer Chassidim Work of ethics, *halachah* and advice authored by Rav Yehudah Ha-Chassid of 12th and 13th century Germany.

Sforno Commentary on the *Torah* authored by Rav Ovadiah Sforno of Italy in the 16th century.

Shaar HaGmul Book by the Ramban on reward and punishment.

Shaar HaTziyun Footnotes authored by the Chofetz Chayim to his work, the *Mishnah Berurah*.

Shaar HaKedushah Name of sections of books devoted to the sanctity of marriage in works such as *Baalei Nefesh* and *Reishis Chachmah*.

Shaarei Dura A *halachah* work widely accepted as authoritative at its time for *Ashkenazi* Jewry authored by Rav Yitzhak of Dura in the early 14th century.

Shabbos Tractate of the *Gemara* that discusses the laws of *Shabbos*.

Shach Acronym of *Sifsei Kohen*, the title of one of the major commentaries on *Shulchan Aruch Yoreh Deah* and sections of *Choshen Mishpat*; authored by Rav Shabsei Ha-Kohen of Poland, 1622–1663.

Shearim HaMetzuyanim BaHalachah 20th century *halachah* anthology by Rav Shlomo Zalman Braun of Brooklyn, New York, organized as a commentary to the *Kitzur Shulchan Aruch*.

Shelah HaKodesh Work on ethics and *halachah* by Rav Yeshayah HaLevi Horowitz, 1560–1630, originally of Prague and later of Israel. The acronym *Shelah* stands for the original title of his work, *Shnei Luchos HaBris*.

Shemos Biblical book of *Exodus*.

Shiurei Shevet HaLevi Work on the laws of *niddah* based on the lectures given by Rav Shmuel Wozner, contemporary Rav of the Zichron Meir community of Bnei Brak and one of the senior *halachic* authorities of our generation.

Shulchan Aruch A *halachah* work authored by Rav Yosef Caro of Turkey and Israel, 1488–1575, covering all *mitzvot* in effect in the exile; known as the Code of Jewish Law and accepted as the source of final *halachic* decisions for *Sefardi* Jewry and as the basis for *halachic* discussion by *Ashkenazi* Jewry.

Shulchan Aruch HaRav A *halachah* work authored by Rav Shnayer Zalman of Liadi, 1745–1812, the first Lubavitcher Rebbe; an expansion of *Shulchan Aruch Orach Chayim* and parts of *Yoreh Deah* and *Choshen Mishpat*. Highly respected in all *halachic* circles, this work is considered the most authoritative work in *halachah* by Chabad and many other *chasidim*.

Shu't Achiezer Responsa of Rav Chayim Ozer Grodzensky of Vilna, Russia (now Vilnius, Lithuania), died c. 1940; greatest *halachic* authority of his generation.

Shu't Avnei Nezer Responsa of Rav Avraham Bornstein of Sochatzov, Russia (formerly Poland), 1839–1910; known as The Sochatzover.

Shu't Avodas HaGershuni Responsa of Rav Gershon Ashkenazi (d. 1693), considered the greatest *halachic* authority of his era, who served as the rav of many communities of Eastern and Central Europe.

Shu't Binyan Tziyon Responsa of Rav Yaakov Ettlinger, 1798–1872, rav of Altoona, Germany, who is known for his extensive commentary on the *Gemara* entitled *Aruch LaNer*.

Shu't Chasam Sofer Responsa of the Chasam Sofer, Rav Moshe Sofer, 1763–1839, rav of Pressburg, Austria-Hungary (now Bratislava, Slovakia). The Chasam Sofer was considered the foremost *halachic* authority of his generation.

Shu't Chavos Yair Responsa of Rav Yair Chayim Bachrach, 1638–1702, German *halachic* authority.

Shu't Cheishev Ha'Eifod Responsa of Rav Chanoch Dov Padwa, principal rabbinic authority of the *chareidi Torah* community of London, until his recent passing.

Shu't Divrei Chayim Responsa of Rav Chayim Halberstam of Sanz, Hungary, 1797–1876, known as Rav Chayim Sanzer.

Shu't Imrei Yosher Responsa authored by Rav Meir Arik, 1855–1926, a *halachic* authority of Butchach, Galicia; during World War I, Rav Arik was a refugee in Vienna; he later returned to Butchatch.

Shu't Maharam Mintz Responsa of Rav Moshe Mintz of Germany and Poland, c. 1415 – c.1485.

Shu't Maharam Shick Responsa of Rav Moshe Shick of 19th century Hungary, 1807–1879.

Shu't Mahari Bruno Responsa of Rav Yisrael Bruno of 15th century Germany and Bohemia, c. 1400 – c. 1480.

Shu't Maharsham Responsa of Rav Shalom Mordechai Shvadron (see *Maharsham*).

Shu't Minchas Yitzchak Responsa of Rav Yitzchak Yaakov Weiss, 1902–1989, of Hungary, England and Israel; served first as the head of the rabbinic court of Manchester and then in the same capacity of the *Eidah HaChareidis* in Jerusalem.

Shu't Noda BiYehudah Responsa of Rav Yechezkel Landau, rav of Prague, 1713–1793.

Shu't Pri HaSadeh Responsa of Rav Eliezer Chayim Deitsch of Bonhom, Austria-Hungary, 1850–1916.

Shu't Rav Akiva Eiger Responsa of Rav Akiva Eiger, 1761–1837; *halachic* authority of his generation who served as rav of several communities in Germany and Poland.

Shu't Shevet HaLevi Responsa of Rav Shmuel HaLevi Wozner, contemporary rav of the Zichron Meir community of Bnei Brak and one of the senior *halachic* authorities of our generation.

Shu't Shoel U'Meishiv Responsa of Rav Yosef Shaul Natanson, rav of Lvov, Austria-Hungary, 1808–1875.

Shu't Shvus Yaakov Responsa of Rav Yaakov Reischer of Prague and Worms, Germany, 1670—1733; prolific *halachic* writer and respected authority.

Shu't Tzitz Eliezer Contemporary responsa authored by the Jerusalem *halachic* authority, Rav Eliezer Yehudah Waldenberg, 1917–2006.

Shu't Yabia Omer Contemporary responsa of Rav Ovadiah Yosef, former chief rabbi of Israel; considered by many to be the most authoritative contemporary *Sefardi halachic* authority.

Shu't Yehuda Yaaleh Responsa of Rav Yehudah Asad, 1797–1866, prominent *halachic* authority and rav of several communities in Hungary.

Sidur Beis Yaakov (of Rav Yaakov Emden) A commentary on the *sidur* by Rav Yaakov Emden of Altoona, Germany, 1698–1776. Also known as *Sidur Yaavetz.*

Sidrei Taharah An exhaustive 18th century commentary on the *Shulchan Aruch* laws of *niddah,* authored by Rav Elchanan Ashkenazi, the rav of Shutland, Germany.

Sifra The *halachic Midrash* on the Biblical book of *Vayikra.* This work is also called *Toras Kohanim.*

Sotah Tractate of the *Talmud* whose primary subject is the laws of a suspected unfaithful wife.

Strive for Truth The English version of *Michtav Mei'Eliyahu.*

Sugah BaShoshanim A contemporary work on the laws of the *harchakos* by Rav Eliyahu Shmuel Vind of Jerusalem.

Taharas Bas Yisrael Popular compendium on the laws of *niddah,* authored by Rav Kalman Kahana under the direction of the *Chazon Ish.*

Taharas HaBayis A book on the laws of *niddah* authored by the former Chief Rabbi of Israel, Rav Ovadiah Yosef, who is considered by many to be the most authoritative contemporary *Sefardi halachic* authority.

Taharas Yisrael An early 20th century anthology on the laws of *niddah* by Rav Yisrael Yitzchak ben Eliyahu of Praga (a suburb of Warsaw, Poland).

Talmud Basic work of the Oral *Torah.* Comprised of the *Mishnah* and the *Gemara.* The *Talmud Yerushalmi* was compiled in Israel, as opposed to the more commonly used *Talmud Bavli,* which was compiled in Babylonia. The *Talmud* is often colloquially referred to as the *Gemara.*

Tanach The Jewish Bible comprised of the *Torah* (the five books of Moses), the Works of the *Nevi'im* (*Prophets*) and the *Kesuvim* (*Writings*). The word *Tanach* or *TaNaKh* is an acronym for *Torah, Nevi'im* and *Kesuvim.*

Tashbeitz *Halachah* work by Rav Shimshon bar Tzadok, a disciple of the Maharam of Rottenberg, who recorded his conversations and learning sessions with his teacher while the latter was being held captive for ransom.

Taz An acronym for *Turei Zahav,* the name of one of the major commentaries on *Shulchan Aruch* authored by Rav David HaLevi of Poland, 1586–1667.

Terumas HaDeshen 15th century *halachah* work by Rav Yisrael Isserlin of central Europe.

Tikunei Zohar A section of the *Zohar*; essentially an extensive *kabbalistic* commentary on the first word of the *Torah*.

Toras HaShelamim Commentary on *Shulchan Aruch* laws of *niddah* by Rav Yaakov Reischer, prolific *halachic* writer and respected authority of Prague and Worms, Germany, 1670–1733.

Toras Kohanim The *halachic Midrash* on *Vayikra*. This work is also called *Sifra*.

Tosafos Northern French and German commentators on the *Gemara* of the 12th and 13th centuries who expanded upon Rashi's commentary to the *Gemara*, particularly by emphasizing a style that includes questions and answers, and often quotes differing interpretations.

Tosafos Chadashim An anthologized commentary on the *Mishnah* first published in the early 19th century.

To'afos Re'eim Late 19th century commentary by Rav Avraham Abba Shiff of Minsk on *Sefer Yerayim* written in the 12th century by Rav Eliezer of Metz.

Tshuvos Beis Shearim Early 20th century responsa work by Rav Amram Blum of Hungary.

Tur The first attempt to incorporate all the *halachic* conclusions that apply in the exile after the destruction of the *Beis HaMikdash*. Written by Rabbi Yaakov, the son of Rabbi Asher, c. 1275 – c. 1340 of Germany and Spain.

Vayikra The Biblical book of *Leviticus*.

Vilna Gaon Rav Eliyahu ben Shlomo of Vilna, Poland (now Vilnius, Lithuania), 1720–1797, also known as the Gra, an acronym for *HaGaon Rabbeinu Eliyahu*, literally, the genius, Rav Eliyahu. His profound scholarship is considered to belong in an earlier, holier era.

Wosner, Rav Shmuel A well-known, contemporary rav of the Zichron Meir community of Bnei Brak and one of the senior *halachic* authorities of our generation.

Yad Aharon There are several works by this name. The one quoted in this book by the *Pischei Teshuvah* is probably referring to an 18th century work by Rav Aharon ben Moshe Alfandari, who lived in Turkey.

Yechezkel *Ezekiel* in English. One of the books of the *Tanach*.

Yerushalmi Bikurim Tractate of the *Talmud Yerushalmi* that discusses the laws of the consecrated first fruits.

Yadayim Tractate of the *Talmud* that discusses the laws of washing hands.

Yeshayahu *Isaiah* in English. One of the books of the *Tanach*.

Yesod VeShoresh HaAvodah An ethical work authored by Rav Alexander Ziskind of Horodno, Poland (now Grodno, Belarus), d. 1794.

Yevamos Tractate of the *Talmud* that discusses the laws of *yibum* and *chalitzah* (the laws of Levirate marriage).

Yoma Tractate of the *Talmud* that discusses the laws of *Yom Kippur*.

Yoreh Deah The section of *Shulchan Aruch* that includes the laws of *kashrus* and the laws of *niddah*.

Zohar An early work of *Kabbalah* by Rav Shimon bar Yochai.

Yosef, Rav Ovadiah Former Chief Rabbi of Israel; considered by many to be the most authoritative contemporary *Sefardi halachic* authority.

Zavim Tractate of the *Talmud* that discusses the laws of irregular emissions.

Index

A

B

C

H

I

K

L

M

P

T

U

V

W

Y

Z